The
ALCHEMY
of
DANCE

Also by Leslie Zehr:

The Sacred Art of Dance Journal

The Al-chemia Remedies: Vibrational Essences
from Egyptian Flowers and Sacred Sites

La Alquimia del Baile: El Baile Sagrado como
un Camino hacia la Bailarina Universal

The
ALCHEMY
of
DANCE

SACRED DANCE AS A PATH
TO THE UNIVERSAL DANCER

Second Revised Edition

Leslie Zehr

The Alchemy of Dance: Sacred Dance as a Path
to the Universal Dancer by Leslie Zehr—2nd ed.
ISBN-10: 1978303505
ISBN-13: 978-1978303508

For all our Daughters and Granddaughters

TABLE OF CONTENTS

INTENTION (PREFACE)

In this book I will try to explain, in words, the journey I have taken, the journey that has unfolded for me and many other women. I followed my radar, the distant drummer, and ended up here. I *knew* it was the right path; the unfolding was so natural, so synchronistic.

If I trace it back this journey began for me in childhood. I began dancing as soon as I could stand. Once I could walk with expertise I began studying dance, all types of dance. I would have been a dancer but had the wrong body type for traditional dance.

As an adult I began more scholarly pursuits, first in the areas of health and well being, alternative therapies, bodywork, and finally esoteric wisdom. I studied many modalities with many teachers. I began by accumulating diplomas then working with individual teachers and finally through my own connection to the Divine. I moved from dance to yoga and Tai chi—all of which brought me to this point and prepared me to *understand* all that would be shown to me with greater clarity. Then, having come full circle and armed with information, I returned back to my passion, my sacred fire, my spiritual practice of Dance.

Once I had acquired the information and had the experience I was ready to process all of it and then teach what I had learned. It is always in the teaching that we can truly appreciate what we have learned. Our experience and understanding become externalized when we teach. We can see what we really know and more importantly what we *don't* know.

This Dance is very primordial, very experiential. In the beginning I only taught it as a class, as an experience, and swore that I would never write about it because it was beyond words. Now I feel I need to integrate both aspects, the information and experience, to describe it in order to birth it, to ground it. I am doing that in the writing of this book.

In my own process I had the information before the experience. What I have witnessed in my students is that they need something to ground their experience as a way to expand their understanding. I have cited resources for further information when possible. It is the journey that is the path not the destination. I think it is important to use this book as a form and pursue on your own those areas that really interest you. This will be different for each person.

The purpose of this book is to fill in the gaps. Whether you are one of my students and need more background information, studying oriental dance with another teacher or on you own, or pursuing dance as a spiritual practice, this book can add clarity and another dimension to what you are already experiencing. For those who have never used dance as a spiritual practice I hope this book will encourage you to try it.

The intention I hold while writing this book is that you will understand what I am transmitting to you through the writing process and not just read the words. The written word is the masculine aspect of communication, understanding is the feminine aspect. Try to integrate them both.

In my classes I don't just teach through words and demonstration—I use all aspects of communication. I explain the movements and demonstrate, but I have also learned to guide and teach by transmission. I believe that it is these subtle aspects that make me an effective teacher. In writing this book I am challenging myself to go beyond the limits of space. Why does transmission have to be limited to being in the presence of the person transmitting? If you know I am transmitting the information in this book and you open yourself to receive it, then it shall be so.

Be assured that I have only the best intentions in sharing this information. I feel this is a gift that was given to me and in service to the Divine I wish to share it with you. This Dance brings both wisdom and joy. I hope you will be as moved by it as I have been and that someday we may Dance together.

ACKNOWLEDGMENTS

I have had many midwives to assist me in the birthing of this book and I send much gratitude their way. In particular I wish to thank my babies, Lina & Abdallah, they give me strength. When I see the love in their eyes I *know* I can do *anything*. I am truly blessed to walk this path with them. And a special thanks to my son, for his words of wisdom "Mom, just FINISH this book, and then write another one!"

I would like to thank my mother, Irma Zehr, for all the work she did providing me with illustrations for the book, both the first and second editions. This Dance is very experiential. Being able to at least see some of the concepts in pictorial form brings some clarity. I truly appreciate her Capricorn determination and drive in helping me to manifest my vision.

I would also like to thank Katarina Kratovac not only for her marvelous editing skills but also for being there to support me through all my projects.

And last but not least I would like to show my infinite gratitude to the Divine Choreographer for leading me through this most amazing Dance. Everyday is a wonderful adventure into the unknown.

INTRODUCTION

Movement is Life.

My intention in writing this book is to invite other woman to understand what I now know and we all feel, which is that we need to move. Life is dynamic not stagnant or controlled. Movement is life. Movement is creation and women are the vessels or conduits for creation.

In general I find that women either love to dance with a passion or hate it—the other type of passion. Most women do not feel neutral about dancing. The reason is that it affects us as women on a very deep level. It taps into our fire, our in-spiration.

The Dance I will describe is a simple vehicle to reconnect with the Divine and recreate the primordial waters within yourself. The primordial waters are where the essence of love exists, the undifferentiated, and the unknown, full of potential. This book merely helps that process occur by initiating it on a conscious level.

Think of this book like a seeding process. I am planting the seed through information and my personal experience. I will explain how and why we dance the steps but it is up to you to feel it. To take in the information, nurture it, and let it grow within you so that it may be birthed through your own individual creative process. I am merely giving you the tools; you will use them to create.

This book has many levels. You may connect to it on whichever level you choose. After you work through one level read it again and move to the next level as it unfolds for you. Embrace what feels right for you and leave behind what doesn't resonate. It may make more sense to you later after some of the information has already been integrated. It is a journey, enjoy it. There is no reason to rush and never push your self into anything that doesn't feel right to you.

Instead of looking for facts ask yourself if what I am saying feels true. Instead of challenging the information ask yourself "how could it be true?" In this way you will connect to the truth and extract the essence of wisdom present.

I have never seen myself Dance—nor do I want to. I am too critical of myself. What I have seen is my reflection in other people's eyes when I begin to Dance and that is truly amazing. I see wonder, joy, light—even shock. They are uplifted and that is what I wish to see reflected back at me, not all the details of error and judgment I have about myself. This Dance is about expression not performance so there is no judgment—only joy.

A woman came up to me after a talk that I gave on Sacred Dance. She was gob-smacked. She looked at me and said, "...of all the women on the catwalk, you out shine all of them (when you dance)". She was truly in shock. She witnessed with her own eyes something that went against her own beliefs. A belief that she could find a woman of my size beautiful and especially when I was dancing! Her standard of beauty was obviously that of a "super-model" (which I am not by any stretch of the imagination) and hey I managed to out shine them! Wow! I left her in a state of shock. Reality was out of alignment with belief. Being a witness to that woman's experience was a gift for me. It was a confirmation of what I know to be true, that the light of beauty shines from within. It is not an external form. It is a state of empowerment.

Prepare to be amazed... at your self!

I know what people see when I Dance. What they see is what I feel when I am Dancing, a woman standing completely in her power, filled with light, in complete alignment with the universe—fusion. That is real power. It may seem strange that anything as simple as dancing could evoke such power. But it is not simply dancing. The universe is full of infinite possibilities. We can dance and we can Dance! It's up to you. Anything you do with passion and intention is sacred. And this is sacred dance.

The only time that I am truly comfortable with my body is when I am Dancing. It is at that moment that I am at one with the universe—me existing in my full potential. It is a feeling that is very difficult to describe but one I hope every woman will experience. It is for this reason that I teach my classes, do my lectures, and now am writing this book. I know from experience that this state of fusion is not out of reach to anyone and that sacred dance is an easy way in.

There has been a recent reemergence of dances such as Belly or Middle Eastern Dance. This makes perfect sense if you consider the age we are living in. There will be a reemergence of the Divine/Universal Feminine and Masculine. This will entail a purification of energies before reunification. It is only through strong polarities that you can attain real fusion, an explosion of coming together. Neutrality contains no charge no potential it is...neutral. It is for this reason that people are having strong polar experiences. There is no middle ground, just the extremes.

In order for this reunification to occur the polarities first need to come together within us. We need to reunite the sexual and spiritual energies within ourselves. This can be done in many ways, usually through spiritual practices that do not deny the sexual aspect of existence. Belly dance which really should be more correctly named "Womb Dance" (for the feminine vessel not the location on the body) is an excellent and attainable way to connect to this energy. The movements appear very sexual when used in the context of performance but are actually very primordial and healing when used in a sacred context.

It is one of the few tribal dances that we presently have easy access to. Most esoteric knowledge is shrouded in some type of "entertainment" until the moment when it is safe to unveil itself. Belly (womb) dance has remained alive in the cabarets and among Middle Eastern women—although most of the sacred knowledge behind it has remained shrouded. In Egypt the majority of my students are Egyptian women because they want to understand the deeper more sacred layers of a dance that is already in their blood.

Most of the women doing this type of dance don't know why they are doing it or what they could do with it. They dance for fun, which is already an excellent reason to do it. The sacral chakra is the center of creativity but also our center of joy. Dancing from our center of joy can only bring an uplifting outcome.

Women feel the call, it pulls them. There are endless stories of how women's lives were changed when they began belly dancing. Most of them were in their forties when they heard the calling. At that age, that auspicious moment in our lives during our Uranus opposition, we are consciously ready to reconnect the two energetic serpents (sexual and spiritual). Dance, especially traditional dance, is a very natural way for women to do this.

It is during our Uranus opposition that most people take up some type of spiritual practice. Uranus is pulling the energy through their bodies and they have physically matured enough to handle it. Sacred dance is a very physical spiritual experience. When you can actually feel the energy moving and the connection, it is very easy to accept and embrace the experience. Once the door is open and you step through you move into *knowing*, and once you *know*, once you have glimpsed behind the veil, there is no turning back.

Each of us has our own personal path but there is Divine order and reoccurring patterns. We are each the infinite recombination of these patterns. Like snowflakes, no two humans are exactly alike. We all contain within us combinations of the same patterns and vibrations just as snowflakes are made up of the same geometric patterns repeated over and over again in infinite combinations.

Because of this there are many maps we can follow on our life path to help us to navigate. There are large patterns/order such as the Tarot and Alchemy. We also have smaller more personal patterns of the same order showing us an example of how this all plays out in "real" life. A map will only take us so far, in the end we must always trust our own knowing, our inner voice, to tell us which map to follow at any given moment.

An astrologer friend once told me "Virgo's make maps and opinions". Having four aspects, including my Sun and my life path in Virgo, I have many of both maps and opinions, but let's stick to maps. Virgos also have the ability to see order in chaos, meaning Divine order. The path was easy for me to navigate because I don't doubt it, I know it. Knowing comes from the heart, our connection to the Divine. Thinking comes from the mind, our connection to ego. Although I could not see the path in front of me I could feel it.

This book is a map composed from the journey that I followed and I share it with you. The experience was my personal path but every experience is just a mirror of a higher order. "As above, so below". I would like to present the map, the higher order, but at the same time give you real life examples and information you could actually use if you wish to follow this map. Although the example or variable I am using is sacred dance I believe this form, this equation, can be used in the manifestation of any creative endeavor such as art or music.

The tarot is one map we will use, one equation. It defines the alchemical process using the most basic language, symbols and archetypes (vibrational blueprints). After my initiation at Dendera Temple I began to see all of life in symbols and the underlying patterns and equations, the Divine order. Symbols have the power to carry an essence, a vibration, a concept, information without opinion or judgment, without limiting its expression.

Alchemy is another equation, a symbolic way of presenting the process of transmutation, or moving to a higher energy form. The symbols and archetypes define the components, the specific elements involved; alchemy defines the process, the dynamic aspect. For that reason I have used the form of tarot and alchemy to define my journey.

Even though I am presenting the process in steps I am in no way implying that this journey is linear. It is not. It looks more like a spiral if I have to describe it. Different energies are above each other, following each other, and connecting across space like a bridge. The different energies are activated at different times for all of us. Some of them are activated at birth and have always been vibrating in us. Others will be activated later in life. They may come to us out of order waiting for the last piece of the puzzle to appear. Don't question the process it will unfold and become clear in the end. Just live it to its fullest.

In the end when all the components are in place we are enlightened, vibrating at the highest, lightest frequency. It is like an orchestra playing a piece of music. There are different instruments. Some may be easy to learn others more difficult. We learn them all. We learn the different parts contained in the piece of music and in the end when the piece is played all the parts come together as one, equally important, supporting each other.

I invite you to take this journey with me.

SACRED DANCE

Sacred dance is as ancient as creation itself. Dance is intrinsic to most women as a form of expression. Although many women have become disconnected from this part of themselves. Through sacred dance they can reconnect with this part of themselves. The Dance is meditative, healing, and empowering. It bridges the sexual/spiritual gap that most women have lost. I see it like a perfect "martial art" for women touching all levels of our existence, physical, mental emotional, energetic, and spiritual.

Sacred dance can help women connect to the creative and sacred parts of themselves. This is a dance for women. It is the Dance of the womb (rather than belly). Each time we Dance we can recreate the universe like *Nut*, the sky goddess, swallowing the sun and re-birthing it each day.

The womb is our sacred space to create within. A woman's center of gravity just happens to be her abdomen, her womb, over the sacral chakra. A man's center of gravity is higher up, located over his solar plexus. From that fact alone we can see that our *centers* are physically and energetically different.

At a higher level there is a male counterpart to this Dance. The role of the male is to bring in, hold, and stabilize energy. The woman moves the energy. Together they create the *Dance of the Sun and the Moon*. But first, as women, we must recreate the primordial waters in order to birth both the male and female.

Sacred Dance is dancing for expression
rather than performance.

What makes sacred dance different from other forms of dance, what makes it sacred, is the intention behind it. Our intentions during the Dance are conscious, which intensifies the experience even more! From a healing perspective this makes all the difference in the world. Through our intention we can invoke different energies. We can Dance for healing, celebration, even purification. The more we understand the components, the energy, the alchemy, and the sacred geometry, the clearer our intention becomes. The clearer we are the higher we vibrate. It is the connection and state of mind that make it different from other forms of dance.

Like in martial arts we connect to the source in both direction, through Earth and heaven, the root and crown chakras. Through the root chakra we are connecting directly to the Earth. We can channel healing energy in and discharging unhealthy energy out through the Earth. Mother Earth being the greatest of alchemical vessels then transmutes this energy and cycles it back, thus is the cycle of life.

Some years ago, just after this unfolding began for me, someone sent me an article written about a study that had been done with tribes in Africa. The conclusion of the study was that incidents of cancer had increased amongst the tribal woman as the practice of tribal dance, specifically dancing to heavy drums, had decreased. They found a direct correlation between these two incidents. Although it would take more research to prove that it was the dancing to drums specifically, or exactly which aspect of the tribal dance reduced the cancer, intuitively we can feel the implications of what was found.

My immediate feeling upon reading the article was that it was the discharging through the Earth during the dance that had kept them healthy. Although that may be one aspect, there are so many benefits to this type of dance that we needn't limit ourselves to any one of them.

The benefits are numerous. On a purely physical level it is great exercise. Many of my students noticed that they were sweating and really working but didn't feel it was like "exercise". They could feel the energy moving through their bodies. Moving from the sacral center brought them great joy, which made them *want* to do it.

It is not meant to build muscle but tone the muscles. It does however increase flexibility in very important places such as the spine and lower back. Flexibility is a feminine principle; strength is a masculine principle. This is why it is fairly easy for women to increase flexibility and for men to build muscle but not necessarily the other way around.

The Dance shows a woman why she is built the way she is,
what each of her perfect body parts were intended for,
and how to use them.

This beautiful Dance will change the body creating the perfect goddess body type just by the nature of the movements. Nature is practical and perfect. We should not question this. It was only after doing this Dance that I understood why we (women) are built the way we are. I understood why we have hips, breast, and bellies! No they are not a mistake or something that needs to be worked off or removed. They serve a purpose! It was then that I finally embraced my own body. This is why it instills in us a sense of self-esteem and appropriate body image. The only time I fully embrace my body is when I am Dancing. During that time I find nothing wrong with it, no imperfection, nothing to be fixed. I enjoy the divinity of my perfect female body.

On the emotional level it brings us great joy. Because we are dancing from the womb, our sacral chakra, our creativity center, our center of joy the Dance is fun! It is a great way to release tension and transmute negative emotions. Anger, for example, results from a feeling of helplessness. By finding ways to empower ourselves such as Dancing, we no longer need to be stuck in anger. We have the power to change or transmute the toxic emotion at the most basic level. When we are empowered we are no longer helpless. I use it often to transmute toxic emotions. Just being in that state of *oneness* reminds me that I am part of the greater whole. Any small obstacle I may be encountering is exactly that—small.

Mentally we move into a state of *no-mind*. This is the same state we attain during mediation. It is the state of oneness, a feeling of being completely present, in the moment, and connected. For me it feels like being in love.

Energetically we are moving the Earth's energy through us transmuting and discharging harmful energy. We do this on many levels through different processes using our bodies as the alchemical vessel for transmutation.

SACRED SPACE

Sacred space is an important element in sacred dance, or any kind of spiritual practice. In a sacred space we are free to be vulnerable, permeable and to allow the Divine energies to penetrate and fuse with us. This is not the case in normal or mundane space where we cannot be certain of what kind of energies are present.

In this sacred place we are connected to the greater consciousness that lives always in the present. We perform dances and rituals that connect back to the past and into the future because they are archetypal—always in Divine time.

What is Sacred Space?

It's very important that you keep a sacred space for any kind of deep work whether it be healing, meditation or any of the sacred arts. Any time you are doing energetic work where you're trying to shift energy or you're trying to connect to the Divine, it's important to create a sacred space.

Sacred space is a crucible or womb for our growth—our unfolding. It is the place where transformation takes place. We create a safe space to allow the Divine to be present and to act upon us.

Sacred space is not of this mundane world, it is an opening, a portal to the numinous realm. Think of sacred space as a temple, or a church. It is someplace that's used for sacred work—a place where the Divine can come in and imbue the space. It is a place for the Divine to be honored and revered—a place for the Divine to call home.

What happens when we create a sacred space is that we are showing respect for the process that we are about to embark on.

We're creating a safe space so that the Divine can show itself. It's showing reverence—giving more importance to the whole process.

Sacred space takes on many forms. It could be something that is temporary or shifting, like a place in your home where you are doing sacred work or a treatment room. Or it can be somewhere that is permanent, like a temple that doesn't change. It is not so much the location but what fills the space itself.

What we want in a sacred space is to only let the right kind of energies in. We want to focus on letting the Divine in and to be really clear about that. When we are not clear, then other energies may be free to come in. We need to be able to be permeable in order to be shifted. A sacred space needs to have a boundary in order for us to be able to make ourselves vulnerable.

Space is a feminine concept. The masculine is the boundary and the feminine is the actual space within. This is another concept that has been lost in Western consciousness. We think of "space" as being empty but it is not. It is full of life and potential. Think of a balloon: what fills the balloon may be invisible, but it is what is expanding the boundary of the plastic balloon. In order to imagine the power held in the internal space, think about what happens if we prick the balloon with a pin. Explosion! The potential is released and it is powerful.

In ancient times people used to create sacred space when they settled new lands. The sacred space was often first a country, then a city and then a temple in the center of the city. What they were doing through this act of "settling" was to activate that space. So that it became a space where the Divine was present. They wanted to activate that space so that it worked in Divine time, Divine order.

What is Sacred Time?

When we move into sacred space we move into sacred time. We move from normal mundane space and time and into the numinous realm. Sacred time is out of mundane or profane time—meaning that it's out of ordinary time. In this place we are connected to energies greater than ourselves—we are timeless.

In the coming chapter I will explain the archetypes and how they are primordial waves in the collective unconscious, so maybe we could call this sacred time and space—the collective unconscious. It's the eternal present. It's always there but it is out of mundane time or mundane space. It is eternal time—Divine time.

When we do sacred work, when we connect to the Divine, we move to a different dimension—the dimension of sacred time and space. This is what happens when we move into the state of no-mind, which we're trying to do in the Dance or in any kind of spiritual practice.

Mundane time is man-made, a product of the mind. When we go into no-mind, we release that limitation and move into sacred time where we can be connected to all of time past and future because we are out of mundane space, we are in the dimension of sacred space.

During the Dance, when we move to the place of no-mind we have entered that dimension of no time and no space. We've moved into Divine time. If you have ever had peak experiences in your life, or when you're dancing or meditating you get the feeling of being out of real-time. You feel you're in another place, like you're something out of time—and that's what we call sacred time.

Mircea Eliade called this the "eternal return" or cyclical time. There are eternal cycles or repetitions. Time is not linear. It is not something that is man-made. All events go back to the beginning of time. This is where phrases used in the bible such as "in the beginning" or in fairytales, "once upon a time", came from. They are telling us that the story we are about to hear is archetypal, eternal, it happened/is happening in sacred time.

Sacred time and sacred space are very closely linked. In order to move into sacred time, we have to have a boundary to define and transform mundane space into sacred space—mundane time to sacred time. We have to create a container, a vessel or a crucible.

Why is Sacred Space so Important?

In order for you to allow yourself to be vulnerable or permeable you need something with a boundary, you need a container—a "womb". There needs to be an edge that defines where mundane life ends and the sacred begins. The place where man's will leaves off and Divine order steps in. We define that boundary by creating a sacred space.

It needs to be a space where other influences are not allowed—a place where we are letting only the Divine, benevolent energies in. It is our holy of holies, our temple on Earth for our sacred work.

Use the analogy of a womb. A womb is a protected place, dark and internal, like a cave. In the womb the seed is planted and grows. It is protected, unobserved. It is untouched by the outside world while being nurtured. It moves in Divine time.

The child in the womb does not realize there is any kind of external "timeline". It is in the process of unfolding in Divine time until the moment it is birthed. In modern times we are used to external influences such as induced labor, but if we think about the "natural" process, all moves forward in a pattern of unfolding—without human intervention.

A Place to Be Vulnerable

Vulnerability is one of those words that is negatively charged. People don't want to see themselves as being "vulnerable". But being vulnerable is being permeable. If we want healing or transformation to occur, if we want to be able to be imbued with Divine energy, if we want to be seeded with that Divine energy—we have to be permeable. We have to allow ourselves to be vulnerable to be acted upon.

It is not possible to be vulnerable and protect yourself at the same time. These are two divergent roles. Unfortunately we have been indoctrinated into the idea that we always have to protect ourselves. And unfortunately we do need to protect ourselves because there are energies out there that are not benevolent.

In order for us to go into the sacred time and connect to the Divine we need to be vulnerable. But how can we do that? How can we be vulnerable and safe at the same time? We create a boundary, a container—a sacred space. That way we can allow ourselves to be vulnerable. We can be free. We can be relaxed. We can be open to the Divine energies without fear of harm. We can then create whatever needs to be created or allow in whatever needs to come in.

We need to be safe in order to do that, which is why we create a boundary before we even begin the process. This boundary becomes a threshold, the place that separates the sacred from the mundane.

Temples or churches are considered sacred spaces—permanent sacred spaces that retain the energy of the Divine. Ancient temples always had a gate and usually only one gate. The gate was made out of cedar. Cedar is a wood used for cleansing or purifying. When the initiate passed through the gate, they were cleansed and purified. They were stepping through a threshold.

The threshold immediately creates the intention of moving into sacred space and sacred time. Boundaries have their guardians. In the case of the temples, the cedar gates were the guardians—the protector of the boundary. When the initiates passed through the gates, it was very clear that they moved out of mundane space and time into sacred space and time.

The same is true of sleep. It is a time when we move into another dimension. We become vulnerable anytime we are in an altered state of consciousness; we should be careful of our environment. Whether it is sleeping, channeling, taking sacred plants or Dancing, whenever we are in an altered state of consciousness we need to be in a sacred space—and mind who we allow into our sacred space. Think about whom you sleep with or Dance with.

How do We Create Sacred Space?

Creating a sacred space can be done in many ways—it is the intention and purity of the space that makes it sacred. When creating a sacred space, use tools or rituals that are sacred to you and only ones that you clearly understand. Don't just do something because someone else told you to do it—that does not hold intent or connect you to the past if you are mindlessly going through the steps. And if it does, you may get a reaction that you are unprepared for—so be careful of what you do.

It should be a closed area in the sense that it is like a womb. We need to define the boundary of where it is. We don't want other energies coming in and out when we do sacred work. It should not be a hallway or passage where people will be walking up and down because then you're shifting the energies all the time. Different kinds of energies are coming in so try to create a space that is a closed area.

It should be a place in which you won't be disturbed and you won't be observed. When other people observe you and they are not in sacred time, they are in mundane time; a weird warp in the energies is created. If it is a place that has windows, close the curtains or cover them.

You don't want to be disturbed so close the door, turn off the phone. You cannot be going into sacred time and then jumping out of it. It is something you enter into, it is a ritual and intention to be in that space. Even if you're only in that space for five minutes, you are going into sacred time and stepping out of mundane time for those five minutes—so really honor it as that. It doesn't have to be forever but it has to be clear—the boundaries need to be really clear.

You want your sacred space to be comfortable because you want to relax in it. It shouldn't be too hot or cold. You want to make sure that there's enough ventilation because you are going to be breathing deeply.

I mentioned the temples. The temples usually had a wall around them. The wall was usually made out of some kind of stone. And very often it didn't have windows or the windows were very high. It would let the light in but it wasn't allowing other people to look in. Even in a church you tend to have high windows or stained glass windows. The stained glass lets the light in but it doesn't allow people to observe what is going on inside.

Sacred work is not something that should be observed. If people are in church praying, they don't need to be watched by other people. I think this is a really good analogy—to think about the sacredness of praying and how it isn't a spectator sport.

The same thing is true of the child in the womb. The womb is a closed area. Now we have ultrasound to peer into the womb and see what the child is doing. Now the child can be watched but in nature it is a closed place not to be observed. It doesn't have windows, the light doesn't come in. Seeds germinate in the dark under the ground and then the maturing plant comes through the ground. We're not meant to be watching that process as things unfold. Try to think of your sacred space as a temple or womb. And make it something like that.

Once you've defined where your sacred space is, and you have set it up in a way that you like, be sure to clear it of any intrusive energy. If it is a space that's not used for anything else, then this will be easier, but if it is a space that is used for many things, such as a place in your home that you use sometimes for sacred work or in a center, like a treatment room that other people use, you need to clear it every time you use it. You really don't know what kind of energy was in there before you got there.

When we have a space like a temple that is always used and kept alive by bringing in Divine energies, then we needn't clear the space as often. Even in a temple or church it is an ongoing process. Churches and temples are often cleared with frankincense. It is a ritual that is done before every service—showing the importance of clearing the space. If it is a space that is used for other things, make sure you clear it thoroughly each time you use it.

Always set the intention before you begin. The intention can be as simple as only letting healing energies or Divine energies come in—intrusive energies are not welcome. All kinds of different energies may try to come in, so be clear about what you're doing. This is important. Often people are not clear about what they're doing. One can be very naïve, which I have been in the past. This is why I'm cautioning you about this.

When I used to hold full moon gatherings at the temple, I just assumed that everyone understood that they were in a sacred space and that it was a sacred circle. Then later, I would hear people outside of the circle talking about what happened that night at the gathering or what so-and-so said or did.

It was then that I realized that I had never actually spoken the words out loud: "This is a sacred space, whatever happens in this space stays in this space. Do not invoke any other kind of energies, just allow the Divine energies to be present". I just assumed that everyone understood that so I didn't verbalize it. To create a safe space for people to really go deeply into the process, one needs to be clear and state things that may seem obvious.

I have learned. The space that I use now is different. There are less people that come into the space and I'm really clear about what I do. I make sure that other kinds of energies don't come in. I don't allow people in this space when I don't know what they're doing. I'm much more careful about the space and who enters the space, how I charge the space and how I clear it. "Live and learn".

I've had students say that just coming into the space was a healing event. They could feel the energy—because they feel safe. In order for transformation to occur we need to feel safe. We need to feel like whatever happens is Divine unfolding. And that is the only way that we can be truly relaxed enough to let the energies come in and to be acted upon.

Think of it like a cocoon that a caterpillar builds before it turns into a butterfly. It creates a sacred space to allow itself to dissolve and be reborn. These are the kind of things to keep in mind when you're creating a sacred space.

Dancing in a sacred space is such an amazing experience. Once you have tried it, you will see clearly how it adds to the quality of the work you are doing. Sacred space is something that was very much in the consciousness of ancient people but has been lost in modern times. Through the Sacred Arts we can revive the traditions, reconnect with the Divine, and move back into sacred space and sacred time.

Creating a Sacred Space for Ourselves:
- Use a closed area (in the sense that it's like a womb)
- Don't allow other energies coming in and out while you're doing this work
- Be sure you will not be disturbed or observed
- Clear it of intrusive energies
- Close the door, turn off the phone
- Close the curtains or cover the windows
- It needs to be comfortable so you can be relaxed
  o Not too hot, not too cold
  o Good ventilation
- Set the intention before you begin
  o Only healing/Divine energies are welcome
  o Intrusive energies are not welcome
- Use tools or rituals that are sacred to you
  o Essential oils
  o Smudging
  o Crystal bowls

ALCHEMY, ARCHETYPES AND THE TAROT

Alchemy is basically transmutation of anything through a process of separation, purification, and recombination. The steps are like an algebraic equation that can be applied to almost any transformational process. The principles behind the art and science of alchemy are very simple, transmuting lead (base metal) to gold. Each transmutation has its own variables, which are the lead and gold, but the equation remains the same. In physical alchemy the alchemist is using real physical elements such as lead, acids, plant material, and mercury. In spiritual alchemy the *lead* is our unaware conscious state, the *gold* enlightenment. In the Dance it is the physical movements that take us to a place of oneness, fusion, the Divine—this is our gold.

Like the *Caduceus* (Hermes' staff) the two serpents continuously divide and recombine. The separating is the dissolution, the breaking down. The recombining is the point where we synthesize or integrate the experience. The goal is always the same, to create the Great Work, to know the perfection of life, the Absolute, to become the Universal Dancer.

The tarot is a set of images, pictures, which illustrate the different stages and levels of the alchemical process and the archetypes. The tarot itself produces a kind of transmutation through experiencing the images. The images themselves are primordial and deeply connected to the *collective unconscious*. They work like keys unlocking and initiating processes in the unconscious mind. Working with the tarot in anyway will initiate a process whether we are conscious of it or not.

Although the archetypes are universal, the pictures on each tarot deck are slightly different. They are one artist's interpretation of those archetypes. For that reason I have not included pictures of the individual cards. I suggest that you use a deck that resonates with you. While you are reading the description of each archetype look at the corresponding card. That way you can feel the archetype from the picture as well as reading about it.

At this time we are living in the age of alchemy. Our awareness has opened to the point of truly realizing the range of transmutations at our disposal, physically, emotionally, and spiritually. In this alchemical era we move into the Age of Aquarius bringing times of great change for humanity. The message behind the Age of Aquarius is ascension or destruction.

In astrology we move along the axis from Leo (ego) to Aquarius (humanity), from the I to the we. This is yet another example of the separation, purification and recombination process. In order for humans to be able to move from the isolated, individualized state of "me, me, me", they will have to go through a process of purification to reintegrate them into humanity in order to reach the *gold*.

People, whether conscious of it or not, are presently going through a transformational process, the spiritual evolution. When we move through the process consciously, that is enlightenment, illumination, and awareness. When we move through it unconsciously, that is struggle, strife, and hard lessons. Doing any practice which connects us to the whole, the Divine, will bring us to a clearer sense of humanity removing the feeling of separation.

Our goal is the gold, to become the Universal Dancer, the last stage in the transmutation, the fusion point. At that point the elements no longer exist individually, somehow connected yet easily identifiable as their separate parts, but in a state of fusion where there is no separation. This point of fusion or flow, the Universal Dancer, is the same concept depicted by the tarot and in the Mayan calendar, the state of "Oneness" beyond polarity.

When we remove resistance through a process of purification, we allow that energy to take its highest form. So how does this relate to the Dance? In the Dance the body becomes the alchemical vessel. The transmutation is the energy taking different forms as it passes through our body, the vessel. We can use the energy pulsating from the Earth and transmute it into visible movement. The music becomes the guide or the form that we follow. The Earth pulsates, vibration creates sound and movement. These elements can be recombined in infinite variations creating new music and new dances.

1st Alchemical Stage-"Nigredo"

The first level or step in the alchemical process is *Nigredo*, the physical or Earth level. This stage of the Dance is preparing you to be a conduit for the energy. This is the level that I will present in this book. The preparation involves mainly surrender and flexibility in the body so that when the energy passes there are no obstacles, no resistance, nothing to stop the flow. The more flexible and supple we are the more easily the energy flows. It is an exercise in passivity and surrender. As the first Hermetic precept states, "As above, so below", our ability to surrender physically to the amazing flow of energy passing through our body from the Earth is just a glimpse, an analogy to the incredible energy available to us when we surrender spiritually to become the Universal Dancer.

The first goal in the Dance is to create the primordial waters. The *prima materia* from which all else will be birthed. This *prima materia* already exists in nature and in the archetypal vibrations; all we need to do is tap in or reconnect.

We learned from basic physics that energy cannot be created or destroyed but it can change form. As technology advances and our spiritual perspectives change, we begin to realize just how many forms are available to us.

In most types of spiritual work it is generally accepted that our experiences are what we learn from. The Earth and our bodies are polar and therefore we can quantitate and compare. The Earth and body become our laboratories for experience.

Most of us are very accustomed to experience. We are in a constant state of experience. But the true learning comes not from the experience itself but in the processing of that experience, the separating and then reintegrating of the event. Without processing we tend to just repeat the same experience without learning. This is called "repetition compulsion". We have the same experience over and over again until we "get it"—learn the lesson. Then we are free to move on to a new experience. This is a very slow, difficult, and often painful evolution.

The vessel for the Neptunian environment we are creating, the *prima materia*, is the womb. Power initiates from the womb, the *tan tien* in the martial arts. The womb is our creative center where we house our primordial waters and the sacral chakra.

Once we have connected to the *prima materia* we can begin the first dissolution. We now break the form down into the elements, fire, air, water and earth. In the Dance each movement takes on a different form related to the element it corresponds to.

In this book I will not go through each alchemical process. If this interests you then I recommend that you deepen your studies in alchemy. What I would like to do here is present an over view showing how all these aspects come together. I wish to plant the seed. If something resonates with you then nurture the seed and it will grow.

Archetypes

The other aspect of the tarot that I wish to present are the archetypes. Archetypes in their essence are energy patterns. The vibrations permeate our subconscious so whether you are aware of this or not it still affects you on some level. Carl Jung explained them as residing in the collective unconscious, the universal mind that we all have access to. But there is a deeper level. Before something appears on the mental level (air) it exists on the energetic level (fire).

The archetypes are the vibrations behind the characters in mythology and the tarot. Because they are so essential, vibrational in their essence, every creation story and most mythological stories, even fairy tales, have the same characters. We can all relate to them on some level. The vibration, the energy behind the character, is the same in each story all that changes is the external manifestation, such as the name given to the character/archetype. In this way it is easily integrated into every culture making it personal to the culture. But its universal aspect is the vibration, the subtle level.

In Native American mythology the archetype of the Magician is Coyote, in Pharaonic (ancient Egyptian) mythology he is Thoth, Mercury in Roman, and Hermes in Greek. In each case the energy, the essence, the lesson, the vibration, is the same only the name changes. The Magician is one of the greatest teachers, a messenger of the gods. He teaches using the elements. Because he has full knowledge of the elements he can manipulate them, often using that as a teaching tool. He is a prankster, a trickster, showing us the skill of manipulation and illusion.

Archetypes are also present in astrology. When we prepare a natal chart we can see all the archetypes present and vibrating within us. These archetypes are imprinted on our DNA at birth like a vibrational genetic coding. The frequency we vibrate at is the synergy of all these vibrations.

My initiation at Dendera opened me up to understand the archetypal world or the collective unconscious. I am using the same tool used in astrology or tarot to illustrate this path, the Dance. The reason we can do this is because the vibrations fall naturally into Divine order. What I now know is far beyond the scope of this book and has so many applications that I will limit my discussion of the archetypes to the Dance and encourage you to tune into or study the archetypes in their universal applications. An excellent book on archetypes in relation to spirituality is *Sacred Contracts* by Caroline Myss. I will present a brief overview here and go more deeply into each archetype and its relation to the Dance in the following chapters.

We begin as the Fool, the initiate, the seeker, walking our path in full *knowing* of where we are going, but not necessarily how we will get there, surrendering to the process. The first step is the Magician. The Magician knows how to manipulate the elements. He has full knowledge of the elements and knows how to use them.

Then we move to the High Priestess, she brings in a catalyst, intuition. With this catalyst we begin to come down to the earthly realm, as a messenger. She has glimpsed behind the curtain and has seen the infinite. She moves by intuition being connected to the great *flow*.

The archetype of the Empress is the sacred cow. She represents creation, the creative process, and birthing on the subtle level. From the Empress we move to the Emperor, he is the manifested Earth where the Empress is the subtle Earth. In the Dance the Empress is the subtle Earth that we are connecting into, the vibration, the waves, the creation, and birthing of the Dance.

The Emperor is the amplified beat that we can hear with our ears. In our Dance he would be the drum, the actual rhythm or music, the manifested sound from the wave.

After that we have the Hierophant, the high priest. The Hierophant has studied all the sacred knowledge, where the High Priestess embodies it. Sacred knowledge such as sacred geometry can be added to the Dance. We can dance the sacred geometry adding yet another level to our intention.

From the diagram of the tarot just take notice of the relationships between the archetypes as well. The High Priestess is first paired with the Magician. Later she is paired with the Hierophant as they flank the Emperor and Empress, the two aspects of Earth.

Once we have attained all the knowledge and energies present in the archetypes and elements we bring them together in the actual Dance. The last phase of recombining is the dream of the *sacred marriage*. It also has a subtle and manifested aspect.

Just as each feminine and masculine archetype has both a spiritual and manifested aspects (High Priestess/Empress) (Hierophant/ Emperor) the dream of the sacred marriage has both a feminine (surrender) aspect, the Lovers, and a masculine (control) aspect, the Chariot. Like the yin and yang both these aspects are present during the Dance. There is the feminine side the surrendering to the music, the rhythm of the Earth, and the masculine side using the elements and sacred knowledge with intention. Like the two serpents they intertwine and play.

In the Dance, as in life, we progress from one archetype to another; learning and integrating them all. At the end of this Dance we reach the stage of the Lovers, the dream of sacred marriage. After we have had this vision of fusion we move to the Chariot using our personal power to pursue this dream and to find balance. This is one cycle of the wheel, the first level to the Universal Dancer, which is our ultimate goal.

After we have finished that process we begin again. Like the *Ouroboros* the end is a new beginning, death and rebirth, but at a higher vibration, the second level of order as seen in the tarot. What I teach in this level of the Dance and in this book is only the first line of the tarot, the first level of the alchemical process.

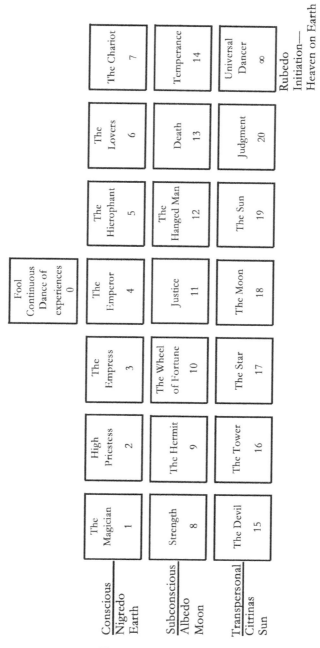

The Magician 1	High Priestess 2	The Empress 3	Fool Continuous Dance of experiences 0	The Hierophant 5	The Lovers 6	The Chariot 7	Conscious Nigredo Earth
Strength 8	The Hermit 9	The Wheel of Fortune 10	The Emperor 4	The Hanged Man 12	Death 13	Temperance 14	Subconscious Albedo Moon
The Devil 15	The Tower 16	The Star 17	Justice 11	The Sun 19	Judgment 20	Universal Dancer ∞	Transpersonal Citrinas Sun

Rubedo
Initiation—
Heaven on Earth

Tarot Major Arcana

UNIVERSAL DANCER

The Universal Dancer is the last card in the tarot. It is often called the Universe or the World. It is the fusion point, the point where we are not just united, but fused. There is no division or polarity. We are one with the universe, flowing, complete surrender and integration.

In alchemy our goal is to become the Universal Dancer, to reach that point of fusion, complete integration, the gold often called enlightenment. In *The Alchemy of Dance* we reach that point through sacred dance, we become one with the music and everything around us. We are in a complete state of no-mind. We do not think about the movements. They move through us. We become them. We surrender to the energy (waves) moving through our bodies and thereby fuse, no resistance.

The Dance itself is an analogy, a way to practice being the Universal Dancer. The universe is holographic, the Hermetic precept "as above, so below" reflects this. The microcosm becomes the macrocosm and vice versa. If we can learn the Dance we can then live the greater universal dance.

Esoteric knowledge is hidden knowledge because of its potential power. When this power is misused it is very dangerous. Through surrender there is empowerment, great personal power from being connected to the Divine. It is power within or moving through us rather than power over others. All ancient cultures practiced this concept of flow and connectedness.

Over time, through the inflation of the ego state and desire for control, this concept was lost. Man wanted to be the Divine, the master of his destiny, and he lost connection and direction. When you can no longer hear the calling of your destiny you try to live another's destiny and will never truly step into your own power, that absolute power designed for only you. All ancient cultures fell because of this desire to control, to become God. The statement "man was created in the image of God" somehow reduced the concept to God to having human like qualities, rather than humans having Divine ones.

The Mayans believed in the concept of flow. Their whole calendar was based on it. It clearly outlines spiritual evolution, Divine order. It emphasizes the concept of being completely in the present, the time and place that it defines is the here and now. When we are guided by our intuition and are always in the right place at the right time.

The Mayan calendar also illuminates the fact that as creation speeds up, our mind, which guides the ego, will no longer be sufficient to handle all the information coming in. In the future we will be forced to use our intuition because it will be the only tool capable of handling the increased speed of the universal dance. Through this evolution our most valuable survival skill will become intuition. Those that have it will survive. They will always be in the right place at the right time, others will not.

Flow is the great lesson of Egypt. It lives in the stones. One must surrender, because there is no other way to live here. If you want to experience the Universal Dancer come to Egypt! Everything changes second by second. The only way to survive in Egypt is to live in the present, in the moment, and feel the next step rather than plan it. Those who refuse, those who live in the illusion of control will not thrive here. In fact this is the reality of life, the greater reality; life is dynamic and ever changing. As I always tell my students "if you want to make God laugh tell him *your* plans".

There is Divine order. The Mayans knew it and all the ancient cultures knew it. We all know it. Just look at nature around you—it is a living example. The trick is to let go of the idea of control and just navigate. As we Dance in-spired using the music as a guide, we also dance through life following the music of the universe. The universe is infinite. We merely limit ourselves by our thoughts and our imagination.

Most of us cannot ever imagine how great something *could* be. We wish for or visualize something incredible. We will probably get it. What I am saying is that wishing is limiting. We could have gotten something infinitely greater but limited ourselves by our small vision.

Why wish for a million dollars when you could have ten million! Give up control and make your intention to receive as much money as you need to do everything that you need to do. I know that this concept works. I am a living example. I never seem to have any money but somehow I do everything I need to do! What is not yours will not come to you. Why pull it in? You don't need it.

There are many paths to the Universal Dancer. One is through sacred dance. That is the path I will present here in this book. The first stage of it is what I call *The Alchemy of Dance*. Like any alchemical process, we can illustrate it by using the archetypes of the tarot.

We have a long way to go to reach the Universal Dancer. Every line of the tarot is just a higher vibration of the one below it. Here we are working at the lowest vibration and translating it into the physical dance. With all its energy and elements, it is still a dance on this earthly plane.

In this book I will take you through the process, step by step, using the archetypes of the tarot to illustrate and initiate you into each step. In any journey we begin as the Fool—the initiate. We have the intention to learn and walk the path, and the courage to throw ourselves into the abyss. The more we surrender and trust the less resistance there is and the closer we move to our goal of becoming the Universal Dancer.

FOOL-INITIATE

We begin a spiritual path or practice as the initiate, the seeker, the Fool. The Fool knows or senses the Divine. The Fool hears the beating of the drum, of her destiny, and follows it blindly knowing, in faith, that it will take her where she needs to go. The card the Fool in the tarot usually depicts the seeker walking joyfully off the edge of the cliff. This is the image of one who follows in trust or ignorance, with *beginners mind*. A butterfly, the symbol of transformation, accompanies her on her journey.

This is the point we all begin from on a spiritual path. We don't know why we throw ourselves into the abyss, joyfully, but we know it is the right step. The Fool is not unaware or someone who has no concept of the Divine. On the contrary it is someone who defines themself as being on a spiritual path. Knowing you are on the path is only the first step, the awakening, the initiation. There are still twenty-one more steps until you reach the fusion point, the Universal Dancer.

From the perspective of the observer, someone who has not heard the call—we must look very foolish. Just like someone dancing wearing a headset. No one else can hear the music, the call of the drum, but the dancer hears it very clearly. Observing someone doing this without any understanding of *what* they are doing—they would probably be thought of as being insane. But that is an external perspective. Everything makes sense given the proper perspective.

In the tarot the Fool carries the symbol "0" (zero). Zero represents the undifferentiated, the womb, which brings us back to the primordial waters. The Fool is the point where we are full of potential. That potential has not yet taken form. It is still undifferentiated.

In the Dance it is the posture that we begin in. In this Dance, just as in martial arts, the position we begin in is called *wu chi*. *Wu chi* actually means undifferentiated, potential, where *tai chi* is the form. *Wu chi* represents the primordial waters the state before form, "0", full of potential.

Before we even think about moving we need to stand. We begin the Dance by standing in stillness, in *wu chi*, building our potential. The feet are hip width apart pointing straight ahead and not turned out. Knees are directly over the feet and directly under the hipbones. The knees are *always* slightly bent. This is the most stable position possible. If the knees are slightly bent then the pelvis will fall into alignment and there will be no pressure on the lower back. We are always over ourselves in proper alignment. This makes us very stable, very grounded.

Once we are completely centered, connected to the Earth and the rhythm, then and only then do we begin to move. When we do begin to move we always move in very small, very centered steps just like in tai chi. Our legs never extend very far out in any direction; this will cause us to be unbalanced.

If you want to move forward, find the correct position by first standing in *wu chi*. Bend the knee by allowing the heel to release from the floor. The knee will move slightly ahead of you. You will still be balanced because your toes and ball of the foot are still in the original position. The hips have not moved. Now take notice of where the knee is. Hold the thigh and knee in place and move the ball of the foot forward so that the shin is perpendicular to the floor. It now falls directly below the knee. This is the furthest the foot should be moved forward. Beyond that point your body will be unbalance. Note that this is only about six inches ahead of its original position.

When walking or moving out of your space always take small steps. This way your body will be over itself. Never out of balance. If you have studied martial arts this positioning will be familiar to you, it is the most stable way to stand or move giving you the most power.

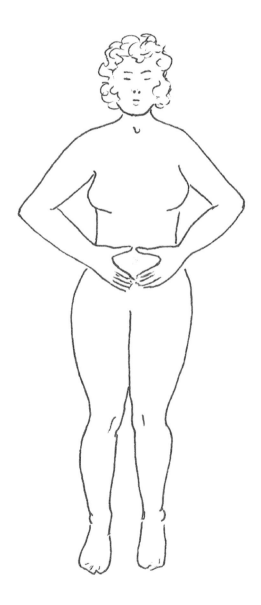

Wu Chi Position Front View

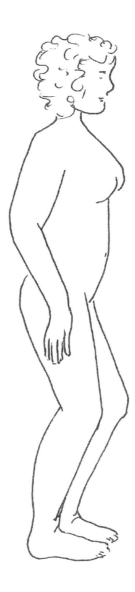

Wu Chi Position Side View

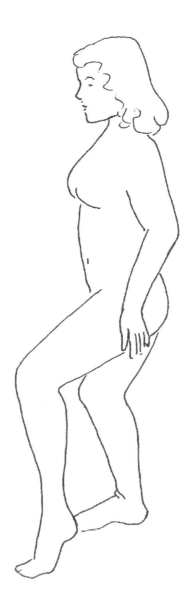

Moving Forward Taking Small Steps

How It Began For Me

This part of my story begins, consciously, in 2002. We were taking our yearly "pilgrimage" to Luxor in Upper Egypt. This tradition had only started a year earlier but it became important for the whole family. For me it was as if everything was finally unfolding. Egypt had been calling me all my life. I had been living in Egypt, in Cairo and the countryside, since 1986. Destiny had gotten me here but somehow I had not yet made the connection to the ancient part of Egypt, the part that had been calling me since my childhood. The reason for that became clear later on. I had been preparing the ground, tilling the soil, for the seeds that were about to emerge.

When I was ten years old I wanted to be an Egyptologist. I, like many people, had a huge fascination and feeling of connection with Egypt. For me I was conscious of it at a very young age. Something was unfolding at that point in my life which often happens around the age of ten. As well as my obsession with Egypt, this was when I had my first *psychic* experience at Teotihuacán in Mexico. How these events are connected remained a mystery until a couple of years ago. But that is another story...

My life in Egypt consisted mainly of being a mother and wife, working part time or studying in the field of healing and integrated therapies (Aromatherapy, Reiki, Homeopathy...). I was running the Women's Center for Health and Well-being in Cairo and exploring the esoteric world, but that was just the tip of the iceberg.

We had devised a beautiful route for our trip by car. We would drive along the coast of the Red Sea all the way down to the town of Quseir. Quseir is known for being the ancient port used by the Pharaohs. It is the shortest distance from Luxor to the Red Sea. There is a highway connecting Esna (just north of Luxor) and Quseir. The drive is beautiful through the mountains. There are ancient mines and hieroglyphs carved on the rocks of the mountains. Unfortunately at this point in time this route is only open to Egyptians. The restrictions imposed on Egypt to keep tourists safe has resulted in foreigners not having free access to many areas. It is very secluded and really out in the middle of nowhere making anyone an easy target. But since I don't really buy into all of that and the fact that we are all Egyptian nationals gave us the freedom to travel this amazing route.

We would spend a couple of days in Quseir on the Red Sea. Then we drove the road west to Luxor. Each trip to Luxor included a visit to Karnak Temple and several visits to Luxor Temple at night. I have a real need to go to Luxor Temple at night. The energy in the temple at night is amazing; it is an experience I would highly encourage.

Luxor Temple by Night

I am very much a night person. Luxor Temple has a lot of bats at night. Bats are one of my power animals; they speak to me on some level—one I could not explain. Bats navigate the darkness and their appearance in your life signifies the onset of initiation and a heightening of ability to navigate the darkness, intuition—something that was very much on the horizon.

As well as visiting the two temples on every trip, we would chose new sites to visit each time. One could spend years in Luxor and still never see everything. This particular trip we decided to go north of Luxor and visit Abydos (near Nag Hammadi) and Dendera Temple.

Abydos was very interesting but didn't really move me. What did move me was being close to Nag Hammadi. It is possible that it was only because of what I know about it historically. The Nag Hammadi Library is a collection of ancient scriptures written by the apostles in which there are many references to Mary Magdalene being Jesus' closest follower. You can feel the presence of Mary Magdalene (Isis archetype) in the whole area, especially Dendera.

When we reached Dendera Temple I felt as if I had come home. Seeing the sculptures of Hat-hor made me happy—not a reaction I expected to have. There are very few pictures of Dendera so it was not a familiarity from having seen it before. A feeling we often have when we see the pyramids or sphinx because they are imagines that we are all familiar with.

Hat-hor's Temple, Dendera

On my very first trip to Egypt, long before I knew anything about the concept of *neter* (*ntr* in hieroglyphs), I bought a silver pendent of Hat-hor, the cow eared goddess. It was the only piece I bought on that trip. She really moved me and I always wondered why I was so enamored with Hat-hor (Taurus) when it seemed that Isis (Virgo) should be the one I am attracted to. I have four aspects in Virgo and only my moon in Taurus.

Hat-hor is the *neter* (archetype) representing the feminine principle, the sacred cow, the matrix, the womb, and abundance. Isis is the *neter* representing the High Priestess/Sacred Prostitute. She is the one who brings in the Hat-hor energy in order to use that energy. A Priestess is a bridge between the vibrational and physical worlds.

Isis was the *Mary* archetype before the feminine energies were unraveled and divided into two. She represented both the Virgin Mary and Mary Magdalene. Virgo (Isis) the virgin retains the original definition of the word virgin—the woman that is whole in her Self, pregnant with potential, but yet undifferentiated. Isis like Mary Magdalene was a Sacred Prostitute/High Priestess and like the Virgin Mary conceived her son without a man, only spirit. Osiris, her consort, was dead, a spirit, not a man incarnate when she became pregnant, giving him the aspect of the *Holy Ghost*.

Five columns with Hat-hor capitals flank the outer Hypostyle hall of Dendera. The hall itself contains eighteen columns with Hat-hor capitals. Also found in this outer hall are representations of the zodiac archetypes. I was in heaven.

Zodiac in Hat-hor's Temple, Dendera

Hat-hor's temple was one of the few temples in which there were High Priestesses and Sacred Prostitutes. It is therefore devoted to all the esoteric arts such as astrology, dreams, dance and others that you can feel but are not defined. Behind Hat-hor's temple is a smaller temple devoted to the *neter* Isis.

Isis Temple at Dendera

Being in Hat-hor's temple was an incredible experience for all of us and a turning point in my life. This was an auspicious moment for me as I was at the peak of my Uranus opposition. The ground was tilled and ready for planting. I was certainly "pregnant with potential". Potential that needed to take form and be birthed.

The Uranus opposition is one of the most important transits in our life, especially on a spiritual/energetic level. It is recognized by many traditions although not named that way. It happens between the ages of thirty-eight and forty-two depending on where the planet Uranus resides in your natal astrological chart.

On the astrological level it is when the planet Uranus is directly opposite where it is in your natal chart. Uranus is the planet of sexual/spiritual energy. The *Kundalini*, the two serpents of energy that lay at the base of the spine, spontaneously begins to move at this time. The reason being that the planet is in direct opposition to where it was blueprinted in your energetic makeup and pulling on you. Moving this energy prematurely can be dangerous and from personal experience very painful!

Although my Kundalini experiences before the age of forty-one were not consciously instigated—they were dramatic and painful nonetheless. After the age of forty-one it became a wonderful expansive experience to feel the energy moving. My feeling is that the body is just not ready for the experience before that. It is not yet mature enough. It would be like trying to impose pregnancy on an adolescent whose body is not fully matured.

Some might reduce this event to "mid-life crises". Carl Jung called it the *Sacred Marriage*. It is the point in which we integrate both sides of ourselves, the masculine and feminine, when the polar energy serpents recombine. In the east it is not generally recommended that one begin Kundalini yoga practices until the age of forty-one. Like puberty this transition is life altering. Once you have passed through it you are forever changed. Your perspectives change and hopefully you move to the vantage point of wisdom.

The Uranus opposition is what begins to shift us into the wise-woman archetype. If we go through it with joy and a sense of adventure it becomes "life begins at forty". If we resist and are not ready for it then it is a mid-life crisis. The choice is yours.

Luckily for me, someone had left me a copy of Barbara Hand Clow's book *The Liquid Light of Sex*. The book outlines the major transits in our lives. It gives a wonderful explanation of what to expect during our Uranus opposition. With this information I was prepared, better prepared, for what was about to unfold.

The process was subtle in the beginning. Many things happened on this trip to Luxor but I was unaware of them until much later when the pieces came together. This process of unfolding, in which the pieces seem to come to us out of order, is very common and I have learned over time to just trust in the process. I know now that in the end I will understand what has happened, what has been building piece by piece. The pieces come out of order but in the Divine moment, when I am ready to embrace the understanding, I am given the key and all the cogs just fall into place.

The night before our trip to Dendera I had a "dream". I did not remember the dream at the time I went to the temple. I remembered the dream months later after other events had occurred to remind me of the dream. It was then that I came to realize that it was not actually a dream but an initiation by the Serpent Goddess.

An initiation is an experience that creates a significant energy shift. The initiation is a door opening. The shift is going through it. We see things differently, experience things differently, or understand things we never knew before without going through the usual process of learning. It is just there, suddenly.

At the time of the initiation I had no basis for understanding the dream. A few months after the experience I met Judy for the first time. God sends little messengers to sort us out, give us the information we need. Judy introduced me to the *numinous* realm, or should I say made me consciously aware of the numinous realm. From there I had a basis for understanding the dream. I also understood that it was not a sleeping dream but an experience on a different dimension. The reason I couldn't articulate the experience even to myself was because the energies were not visible and I was not *doing* anything. I was experiencing, receiving, downloading.

How do I know what happened? It was only after the unfolding that I could trace the events back to that dream. The unfolding would be the confirmation of the experience and give me the understanding necessary to process what had happened to me. After this initiation I was suddenly open to a completely different energy level or dimension, the collective unconscious. A portal (for lack of a better word) was open, direct access. I was not the same as before the experience. Information began coming in. I had skills I hadn't had before the initiation. I could trace it all back to what happened on that day. I have since heard stories of others who had similar experience after visiting certain sacred sites in Egypt.

Suddenly, after the initiation, I could read symbols, archetypes, and any kind of signs. I had dabbled in astrology and tarot since I was twelve years old but could never "get it". There was far too much to remember, too much to memorize. I seem to have an aversion to memorizing. Now I know why, because you don't need to! All the knowledge is out there all we have to do is learn how to tap into it and everything is available to us. This is one of those situations where we understand the wisdom of those rebellious seeds planted within us. It is Divine wisdom not allowing us to go down the wrong path to learn useless skills.

After that day I could look at any symbol and know all that was contained in it. This is why we use symbols to begin with; they are limitless and dynamic unlike language. Language is limited by definitions and cultural understanding, making it static and fixed. Symbols are universal, portals themselves, a way to greater understanding. I believe we all have this skill to "tap in" hardwired into us but through our indoctrination and programming as children we are taught to shut it down. The initiation I had was merely removing the veil so that I could see clearly. I could read the symbols present in the tarot, astrology and dreams—things I hadn't seen before. The skill came in a second. The confidence to use it took time. The process of accepting and embracing what had happened took a very long time.

As always, our best tool for understanding experience is the body. My understanding is that we were given physical, polar bodies, in order to quantitate. In order to have the proof we need to manifest. Manifestation is physical. It is slowing a vibration down to the point where it is heavy and dense enough to gain physicality, so we can see it.

Adam wanted to be incarnated so that he could understand, prove, or to confirm externally (he already knew God in his heart). He lowered his vibration in order to see externally, manifest and quantitate.

We find this principle in tai chi. In order to experience and separate we slow it down. The mind can only process twenty-four frames per second so in order to be conscious of an experience it needs to be slowed down, separated. This is part of the alchemical process to separate out.

My initiation, or the result of the experience, began to manifest in my body. That was how I could see what had happened to me, to be conscious of it and to physically feel it.

Our experiences give us Confirmation not Information. Knowing comes from within.

After the initiation I began having strange physical experiences. The first thing I noticed was movement in my body, movements that I was not instigating. I would be sitting and suddenly feel as if someone had just pushed me.

In 1992 we had a very bad earthquake in Egypt. It started with a bang and that same jerking feeling. We have had several less sever earthquakes since then. Every time I felt that strange nudge I would think it was the beginning of an earthquake. I did what I always do in these situations; I look at the chandeliers for confirmation, to see if the room is really moving. If it is an earthquake they are swinging.

Well, they were not swinging! We didn't have any major earthquakes to my knowledge during this period of time. Ok, it was not an earthquake, perhaps muscles spasms, or a loss of balance?

This continued on quite regularly. One day I was sitting with a student of mine. She and I had done a lot of work together over the years. I was in the process of initiating her as a Reiki Master. I felt the nudge and very discreetly glanced up at the chandelier. Out of the corner of my eye I could see that she was also looking at the chandelier. I turned to her and said, "you felt that?" She looked at me in horror. "Yes! Did you?" So what I was feeling was not inside of me, it was external and was affecting both of us. She went on to explain that she gets this sensation every once in a while and thinks that we must be having an earthquake. So it wasn't just me!

This information made the experience even more curious to me. What was this collective feeling? The Earth? Perhaps a mild earthquake? The sensation was the same as the earthquakes I had experienced but it didn't seem to be affecting the objects around us. Animals can detect earthquakes long before they ever register on the Richter scale. Maybe we were becoming more sensitive to the Earth, like the animals?

At this same period of time another phenomenon of bodily experience was occurring. Often when I would lie down for my *siesta* in the afternoon I would feel my body writhing. This sensation was very different from the "earthquake" sensation. It would happen just as I was drifting off to sleep, when my body was relaxed enough, and my mind had taken a break long enough to allow it to happen. I would catch myself doing this. Like when you catch yourself just before you fall in a dream. I would suddenly come to consciousness and think "what the hell! I'm going to sleep and my body is *moving*?" It wasn't just moving it was dancing! The sensation was as if I was moving to the rhythm of drums, a drum far off in the distance. When I came fully to consciousness I was aware that there were no drums playing, but in this liminal state I could *feel* them and my body would move.

This, coupled with the other experience, convinced me that I was feeling the rhythm of the Earth. She was pulsating and I could now feel the pulse. I was convinced that I had had some kind of attunement. I had never been able to perceive these subtle Earth rhythms before. Something had changed. It was then that I realized that it had all started after my trip to Dendera.

Around the time this was all happening, I received and email from a friend. She had forwarded an article about tribal dance. The article was about a research project. The research was done with tribes in Africa. They linked the rise in incidents of cancer amongst the women of the tribe to the decline of tribal dance. The researchers believed that the dancing, to drums in particular, caused a connection to the Earth, which was very healing. When women stopped dancing due to lifestyle changes their health declined.

This made perfect sense to me. I knew this to be true. We take in energy and more importantly discharge back to the Earth. The Earth is able to transmute these energies in a way that our bodies cannot.

The drum is used to amplify the Earth's rhythm. Musicians, especially drummers, are tuning into the Earth rhythm. This is where beat originates. The drums amplify the Earth's rhythm in order to coordinate the dancers with the beat of the Earth to make it a collective external experience.

It was the pulse that encouraged me to dance. All of this movement and energy moving through me was invigorating. I would dance every chance I got, usually three to four times a day. Mainly the type of dance that was emerging looked like belly dance. Yet in a way these were dances I had always known and done, since childhood.

My mother told me that when I was a child in Perú, as soon as I could stand I learned how to turn on the radio. I would stand in front of the radio and just bounce to the Latin music. She was amazed and thought it was really funny. This makes perfect sense to me now. I was aligning with the Earth's rhythm by *bouncing*. Bouncing is actually an important part of the dance we do. Seems I am back where I started from—the wisdom of children.

During this time of excessive dancing I danced alone. Well, at least until "*the* day". Egyptian women begin belly dancing from the time they can stand (as I did to a Latin beat I suppose). It is just a part of the culture, like in tribal cultures. I remember my daughter belly dancing at my brother-in-laws wedding. She was a year and a half. Someone put her up on the table and she just danced. She was actually better than the very famous belly dancer that was hired to perform at the wedding. I thought to myself "I wish I could do that". It is so natural for Egyptian women to do it, because they have always done it. They don't learn it. It is just part of being a woman in Egyptian culture.

It is always easy to spot a foreign dancer here in Egypt. Not so much by the way they looked but by the way they dance. There is something *unnatural* about it. It is too controlled, hard to describe but easy to see. Although it is customary for women to belly dance together at weddings I knew I would be spotted immediately as an outsider, a *hawagaya* (foreigner). That is not the kind of attention I want! Better to dance alone and enjoy it rather than spoiling the fun by being judged by everyone around you.

Well all that changed when Pluto crossed my ascendant! That happened only a few months after my Uranus opposition. When Pluto crosses your ascendant you always lose something. When asked later by a friend "what did you lose?" my immediate, unconscious, response was "my inhibition".

It was a balmy night May 2002. We were vacationing at the Red Sea again. For some reason we decided to go to the disco tech. I think the kids wanted to go and see what was happening. My daughter loves to dance. I think she and I danced together most of the night. At one point I ended up dancing with my husband.

The music changed, it was Shakira, one of her first hits with a very oriental beat. The rest is history; someone else will have to tell the story, because I really don't remember what I did. All I remember was sitting down at the table with my sister-in-law after it was all over. She turned to me and said in amazement "you're a very good dancer". It was at that moment that I *woke-up*, came back to reality. "Oh my God! What did I just do?" I had been belly dancing in the disco, in Egypt! In front of everyone! All I remembered was all the waiters clapping and encouraging me. The rest is a blur. That was it, the break-through moment, and I have been dancing everywhere and anywhere ever since. Now, to everyone else's amazement.

This experience for me was a real slap in the face, one that brought me to consciousness. Once I had gotten over my inhibition I was ready. I had the information. But the door had been closed. What I knew had no outlet to be expressed. Pluto helped me overcome that obstacle and open the door.

After this release I began teaching dance at a friend's studio in Cairo. I was teaching Salsa and belly dancing to women. I called it belly dancing at the time because that was what most of the women wanted to do. The class was predominantly Egyptian women. I felt I was really there to encourage them rather than to teach them anything. Most of them had been dancing since birth. What could I tell them that they didn't already know? What unfolded was unexpected.

They didn't know how to dance. They knew a few moves. Usually they had one move they did really well. I filled in the gaps and brought in new levels of awareness. In moments of shock I would ask myself, "What are you doing? What are you saying? How do you know this?" I didn't know how I knew it, but I did. I could even explain why the information was true. I doubted myself but they never doubted me. They *knew* that I *knew* what I was talking about, even if I wasn't convinced.

Many of them couldn't really hear the music. I am still amazed at how many people can't hear a beat. I wonder what the implications are of being so far removed from the Earth's rhythm. Once they had confidence in me, or should I say I had confidence in myself, then the healing began. It is the resistance that stops the flow. Once the resistance is removed anything and everything is possible.

Women began reporting back the results of what we were doing. This was the confirmation I needed. One woman had severe back problem and had been to doctors and physiotherapists, nothing had helped. This was helping. She was so impressed with the results. Another woman had a complete emotional release after the class. She knew it was from the dance. Something was releasing from her sacral chakra. I was getting confirmation at every turn. We were still just "belly dancing" but so much more was taking place on other levels.

I continued to do most of my dancing alone when I wasn't teaching. I danced everyday, several times a day if possible. It was at this point that dancing became the Dance. As I would Dance information would come to me. I would open a notebook before I started Dancing, something I still do, because I knew I would get some kind of information. I didn't want to process it in that moment just bring it in. Later, when the Dance was finished, I would look at the information and process it to understand what had been shown to me.

43

I am a Virgo (four aspects in Virgo!) as well as having a Taurus moon. I am very grounded and integrity is a big issue for me. I cannot just take information from the ethers and teach it and expect people to believe me *just* because it came from the ethers! Many things come from the ethers, not all of them good.

I needed confirmation. Before doing all this work I set up the intention that I wanted to understand what had been given to me. I knew it was true. I could feel it. But I needed to know *why* it was true in order to share it with others and stand in integrity about what I was saying. "Ask and ye shall receive". We always get what we ask for; we just often forget to ask.

I Danced and received information. Before I could even begin to think about where I might find facts to support what I had just received—it was in my hands. Friends, or strangers, would call on the phone and say, "did you know that..." Actually yes I did know it but I didn't know why. I thanked the Divine for sending me messengers to confirm, or sight resources for, the information I had received. Wow, life is so simple, we just make it difficult. Until now this is the way I work, which is why the process unfolded so quickly and perfectly. I could never get that much done if I had to go out and look for the information. It just comes to me!

After I received the confirmation I needed I was armed with new things to tell my students, as well as the facts to support it. They would further confirm, through their experiences, the benefits of this information. The cycle would continue and grow. From there I developed the course *The Alchemy of Dance*. The course is merely the process as it unfolded for me being passed on to others. I am merely the Scribe—the one who translated it from experience into a course.

Generally I get information out of order. I just hold on to all the pieces of the puzzle until the key to unlock them, or order them, is given to me. Then it all falls into place in the most amazing way. I understood from the very beginning that this work has three levels. *The Alchemy of Dance* being the first level, which follows the first line of the tarot.

In the summer of 2005 the first level was complete and birthed in form. From there space was opened to gestate the second level. Pieces come in one at a time. And when the process is finished, in the Divine moment, the next two levels will be birthed.

This book is the story up to now. I have hesitated to write it down. Only because this experience, the experience of transformation, is not something you can read about it needs to be experienced on all levels. But what I feel now is that I need to birth this piece in order to make room for the next piece. That it needs a physical form to hold the information. I need to tell this story once more in this book and then close the book and move on to what awaits me next, to move forward rather than to keep repeating and looking back.

THE MAGICIAN (the tools)

The first step on this alchemical path is the Magician. The gift of the Magician is that he knows how to manipulate the elements (fire, air, water & earth) or substances. This is the first separation, distinguishing one element from another and knowing the power behind each one. This process may sound very *magical* but actually it is quite mundane.

We use this process in everyday life and in science, which on some level is supposed to be far removed from magic. A scientist, like a Magician, knows the laws of the universe, the laws by which substances operate. Once we know and understand them we can use them following their own natural order—sympathetic magic. We can then use the energy inherent in a substance or process in ways that make the most of this power. This is not magical but practical. The magical aspect comes in our perspective, the eyes that we are observing through. This will depend a lot on which level we are operating on. For now we will stick to the purely physical level. It is enough.

In the laboratory the scientist uses the laws of physics to predict or manipulate outcomes. The Magician does the same. A stage magician is very familiar with the laws of space, time, optics, and reflection. All of which are very *physical* or low level vibrations. How he creates magic depends on how he manipulates or uses these properties and whether others are aware of what he is doing. Their ability to see and process what is happening in front of them.

In everyday life we use physical laws to do our own manipulations. The more we know about the elements and substances the more we can do. For example most of us know how to use heat (fire) to transmute substance. We can easily change matter from one state to another. If we heat water it boils and produces steam. We have transformed a liquid into a gas. Something most of us do every day. It seems very simple. It is if you know what you are doing. To someone who has never seen this happen it would be quite amazing, perhaps even magical.

The magical becomes mundane when you know or can see the process behind the transformation. Our first level of operation is to understand the physical laws and properties inherent in the substances we are working with. The more principles we know the more we have at our disposal.

The process of spiritual evolution or psychic awareness is mainly a process of removing the veils. Everything already exists in the universe we just can't see it or we block it out. One of the brains main functions is to produce filters. People with few filters are usually labeled as having Attention Deficit Disorder. Within the evolution of consciousness, as our awareness and perspective changes, we will need to revaluate where the norm actually stands.

In most tarot decks we see the Magician represented by a man holding his wand (link to power) next to a table with the four tools. These four tools represent the four elements Wands (fire), Swords (air), Cups (water) and Pentacles (earth). He is indicating mastery over these elements by displaying his tools.

In the Dance we also use the elements of fire, air, water and earth, as well as the polarities of feminine and masculine (negative and positive, yin and yang). Before we can use the elements or dance the moves, we need to learn and understand them. We need to master them so that we can use the power inherent in them to achieve our goal within the Dance.

Polarities

The polarities can be named in several ways, feminine/masculine, negative/positive or yin/yang. They are called polarities because they are at opposite ends of the poles, the two extremes. In the physical world they are usually recognized as positive and negative. One of the important qualities of polarities is that they are electrically charged. The fact that they are electrically charged also means that they are magnetically attracted to each other. This is the *real* law of attraction, where opposites attract. In order to create balance there must be equal amounts of both either pushing or pulling against each other.

Our goal is never to neutralize the polarities but to balance them. We need both extremes. Imagine where we would be if atoms decided that they didn't want to be polar or extreme and decided instead to be neutral! Basically the universe as we know it would cease to exist. We are not looking for neutrality, we are looking for balance. This is why in shamanic thought we are looking at the space between things, the interface. This place is the most dynamic and the most balanced place. It is very magnetic and active, not neutral.

Lynne McTaggart in her book *The Field* explains it very well. She points out the need for both extremes to be present. Her example is the importance for both order and chaos to exist at the same time. She calls it *coherence* when there is a balance between these two extremes. Coherence is an excellent way to describe this principle because it implies that there is intelligence behind this state of being.

When I speak of polarities I like to give them an electrical charge, positive and negative, rather than making them personal by using terms such as masculine/feminine or male/female which is their manifested form. Below are just a few of the properties that we can consider when working with the polarities.

Positive (+) – male, yang, active, manifested
Negative (-) – female, yin, passive, receptive, subtle

The Four Elements

We have four elements we will work with, fire, air, water and earth. They can be looked at in many ways. In science we have different states of matter, different densities, such as ether (fire), gas (air), liquid (water) and solid (earth). There are many ways to define the elements. Once we understand the principle behind them we can use them in a variety ways. Listed here are just a few aspects. There are many books and traditional wisdom that can take you deeper into working with the elements. Here we will just present the form and give you an idea as to how to proceed or where to look. The rest is up to you.

Fire: South, transformation (death/rebirth, destruction/creation), purification, ether, inspiration, passion, energy.

Air: East, ascension, gas state, mental realm, flight.

Water: West, fluidity, adaptability (taking the shape of the container), liquid state, emotions.

Earth: North, manifestation, solid state, earthly realm, physical body.

The Dragon

The symbol of the Dragon represents the four elements joined together, a composite, which is why they are often associated with the Magician. The concept of "slaying the dragon" is mastery of the elements.

My first conscious shamanic journey involved meeting the dragon. This experience happened many years ago before I had any knowledge about shamanism and journeying. It happened spontaneously but I was very conscious of what was happening while it was happening. I had encountered the dragon once before, after my Reiki Master attunement. This experience was quite different.

I first found myself in the darkness. Then a hole began to open, like a portal. As I looked through the portal I could see into a cave. The more I looked through the portal into the cave the more I was moving through it, into the cave. It was very dark so everything appeared in black and white.

Until now I can still see the cave very clearly. As my breathing changed things became clearer. Even though I had never had this kind of experience before I wasn't afraid. I felt fine, and the journey was amazing. The deeper my breathing the clearer the vision became. I went deeper and deeper into the cave.

There seemed to be an upper level, like a ridge, and then a lower level, the floor. The floor had a huge rock protruding upwards. When I entered the cave I was on the upper level, but climbed down to the floor. I still didn't know why this was happening or how I ended up in this cave but I was curious and wanted to explore.

The deeper I went into the cave the more I realized I was not alone. I knew the dragon was in the cave hiding behind the rock. I could not see him, but I could hear him breathing. I continued deeper and deeper into the cave, aligning my breathing with his.

The dragon is a symbol of power. By knowing and aligning ourselves with the laws and elements in the universe we become one with the infinite and this is true power, in-powerment.

The *knowing* that came from this experience was that as long as I didn't go into fear, which is driven by the ego, the dragon would not hurt me. The power would remain empowerment. The only thing that will ever limit me is my own fear, which could cause misuse of this power.

We all have access to all knowledge as long as we do not fear what we will learn or where it will take us and as long as we use it in alignment with the natural or Divine order. The dragon may seem fearful but he is not. It is only the fear within us that makes him so. Having the courage to face ourselves, what is deep in our own cave is what sets us free. Once we know the elements deep within, we will know everything in the universe.

Primordial Movements

Like the Magician, before we can use or manipulate the elements we need to know them, to understand how to use them. The elements of the Dance are the actual movements. There are four basic, what I call primordial movements. They are all wave patterns and are related directly to the four elements. They also define the four basic directions of movement front to back, side to side, up and down, and through.

The most primordial shape is the circle. And as we saw in the previous chapter the Fool represents zero, the undifferentiated in our model. Out of that first primordial shape, the circle, we can form other shapes such as the wave, the spiral and of course the infinity symbol. We will talk more about these shapes but what I want you to notice at this point is that the wave is a perpetual circle that moves out of itself. It is a curved line that if it turned back on its self would form a circle. But we can also take this curved line and move it out into space. When we do this we have a wave.

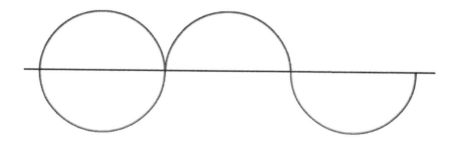

Circle Moving into Wave

When we speak of movement we are usually talking about waves. And as we know most things in our universe move in waves. We have light waves, sounds waves, the ocean moves in waves. Moving through space from one point to another, we use waves, shifting and rebalancing as we move through space. The wave takes us from one point to another whereas the spiral moves us through different levels or intensities. In a spiral we always return to the beginning again but at a different level or intensity.

The four primordial movements of the Dance are waves. The waves move in different directions, on different planes (orientation in space) with different *frequency* (speed, number of waves in a given distance or time) and *amplitude* (size or height of the wave), but they are all waves nonetheless.

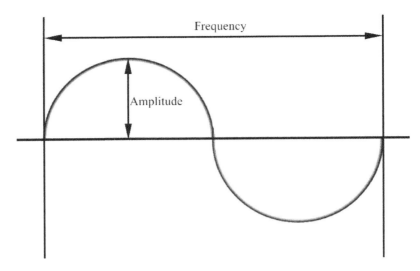

Amplitude and Frequency of Wave

Take a moment to familiarize yourself with the terms amplitude and frequency. The concepts become important later on when we are moving from large waves to vibrations. As you can see from the figure below when we increase the frequency, move faster, we need to decrease the amplitude, size of the wave. Don't try to do very fast movements very big.

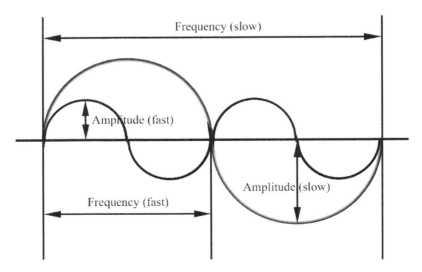

Comparison of Slow and Fast Wave

When we come to actually do the Dance we will use many variations. But before we can do variations we need to begin with the basics. The elements of the Dance, for this Magician, are the four primordial movements. Once the moves become second nature they will immediately resonate with the waves of the music. It is at that point that we will move to a higher level.

Obviously there are an infinite number of variations of these primordial moves individual to each person, for different occasion's or different music. The Dance that I teach looks very much like oriental or belly dance but you will recognize these primordial movements in every kind of tribal dance because ultimately we are resonating with the waves of the universe.

If I were to present the same movements in a different context they would still look very natural in that form. Because they are primordial movements they can translate into any form. This is the form that I learned, the one that most resonates with me. It is also one that has gained popularity in recent years. Because of this, most people are at least somewhat familiar with what it looks like. We see the same elements in all tribal dances be they Native American, Latin American or African.

The primordial movements themselves are not complicated. In fact they are very basic to our nature anyone can do them. The problem is not in the movements but in us. Most of us have stopped moving naturally. We have been told to pull up or hold in—postures that are actually very unnatural and even harmful to the body's structure. Children can learn the movements very easily because they have spent less time holding and repressing the body's natural movements than adults.

When a woman walks it is very natural that her hips should swing from side to side. In western society that is considered sexual or even rude. "Nice girls" don't walk that way. In fact it is the way the body is meant to move. We have become very repressed in the way that we hold ourselves. I have found in my classes that the most difficult thing for a woman to do is to let her hips and buttocks move!

Once the woman does let go of this *holding* she often has an emotional release. It is not uncommon to see women cry—or return to the class with a tale of complete release. Of course they release, the serpent has finally been let out of its frozen cage after all those years of repression! The energy is finally free.

You need not be a dancer or have any dance experience to do this type of Dance. In fact it is often more difficult for women who have been classically trained in dance to do this type of Dance. Most types of dance are based on control and strength; this dance is based completely on relaxation and flexibility.

By connecting to the Earth's rhythm, the waves it emits, the movements flow naturally. It may seem awkward at first because it is not something that most people outside of the Middle East grew up with. The key is to connect into the Earth. The Universal Dancer is truly universal meaning not particular to any specific culture. In time it will not seem foreign, once you realize it is coming from Mother Earth, which belongs to all of us.

Because the movements are rhythmic they actually cause the body to relax. Therapies such as *Trager* are based on the principle that rocking or slight vibration will eventually cause the body to release and surrender. If we keep rocking or vibrating the body at some point it hits a threshold, its *natural frequency*, and just releases. When this happens you will feel the root chakra open/release—an amazing feeling. All of this happens by doing something as simple as just rocking and relaxing! Something children just do naturally.

The Movements

As I mentioned previously the four primordial movements are all different types of waves. The four movements are directly related to the four elements in nature. There are many levels to the four movements but at this stage, the Magician, we are mainly focusing on the physical level, which is what the movement looks like.

The easiest way to describe the movement is by explaining what type of wave we are using. We will look at how the wave is moving and in which part of the body. In the coming chapters I will go into the deeper levels of what the movements do for us. For now we are focusing on how to begin to generate these waves through our bodies.

Another way to describe the movements is through analogy, to do that we will relate the primordial movements to animal movements. Animals are very simplistic—meaning that their movement is in character with their nature. They don't over do or change their movements. They just move in relation to the type of body they were given, functional in a sense.

The use of animal movements will have a deeper significance as we move to higher levels but for now we will just imitate the animal's movement in order to understand and use the elements we are trying to grasp. This is similar to what is done is tai chi. I have named each movement by the animal that it is related to.

As you will notice the animals we have chosen, when combined, bring us back to the dragon. This is not a coincidence. The symbol of the dragon is an illustration of the combination of the four natural elements (fire, air, water, earth) as well as four primordial moves (snake, bat, fish, lion). Please note that the dragon is a composite, a joining together of the elements, but not fusion like the Universal Dancer. In the dragon the parts, although joined, still posses their original character. The original source is very distinct and obvious. Fusion is still a long way off. In fusion there is unity. There is neither separation nor distinction.

What the Movements Look Like

Because we are focusing on the sacral chakra most movements either originate from or gather in the womb. For this reason it is best to begin by focusing on the pelvic area. As the movements become more familiar it will become easier to expand the movements to allow the wave to pass through the entire body.

Loosening of the body often takes time. We are programmed to hold the body in place. Depending on how old you are, you may have been doing that holding for a very long time. In order to do this Dance we need to reprogram. We need to activate the feminine principles of flexibility and receptivity. The muscles must be soft, not contracted, in order to let the energy flow through them.

This loosening may take some time to get use to. We must practice letting go. The objective is not to force something to happen but to relax into it. To empty ourselves out in order to remove all resistance so that the energy is free to pass through us, move us, and guide us unobstructed. This is quite contrary to what we learn in most other kinds of dance. In other types of dance we practice in order to gain more control over the movements.

For this reason it is important to first learn the primal elements of the Dance. This will give us direction and a modality for acquiring this new way of moving. We will be allowing movement to move through us rather than forcing or controlling it. Although the movements are very simple and natural, they may, in the beginning, be difficult to relax into. Your new mantra will become "relax, relax".

Remember to always begin in the *wu chi* position. This is the most balanced and centered position that we can stand in. To allow the wave to move properly through our bodies we will have to be very centered. A lot of energy will be moving through our bodies. We need to be centered enough to handle it. In all four of these movements we will remain in the *wu chi* position.

The knees are always slightly bent—**never** locked. Energy cannot move through contracted muscles. Even when we straighten our legs, the knees are still soft, slightly bent. All the joints are soft, never locked. As long as our joints are slightly bent we will always have somewhere to go. When the joints are straightened, or even worse locked, we have reached the end of the movement. Because this Dance is fluid one movement moves into the next. The way to insure continuous movement is keep all the joints soft.

Snake: The first movement is called the snake and is related to the element of fire. This wave takes on the characteristic of the snake when we are doing it. The wave moves through our body from our feet up to the top of our head. The plane we are working on is side to side.

Begin by raising one hip up and then the other one, alternating from side to side. Obviously if one hip is up the other one has to be down because they are connected. Once you have raised one side all the way up then focus on the hip that is down and raise that one, alternate from side to side. As always, the trick is in the knees. As long as your knees are bent, even slightly, you have flexibility to move.

In time the body becomes more and more relaxed. When this happens the waist will become more flexible and the movement will begin to move through the whole body, from the hips to the waist, up thought the ribcage and then the shoulders, neck, and head.

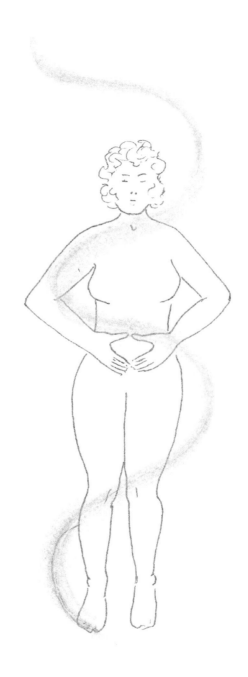

Snake Wave Movement

Bat: The second movement relates to the element of air, and is called the bat or bird. I prefer the bat for reasons I will mention later but either animal moves in a very similar manner through the air. Visualize the one that most resonates with you or use the qualities of each one where it best fits.

Bat Wave Movement

Air is light. We fly through air. We move through air with our arms as the bat uses her wings. For us our "wings" (arms) actually originate from our shoulder blades. We move from our shoulder blades. This is very important. The correct positioning here is with our shoulder blades touching.

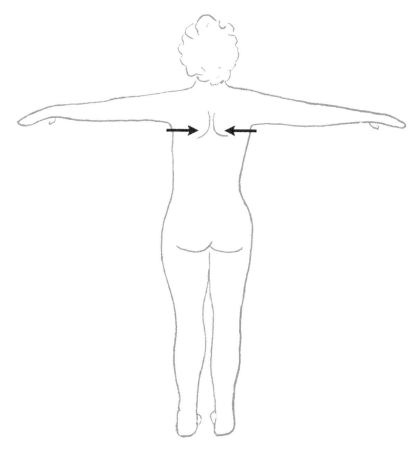

Bat Posterior View. Shoulder Blades Touching

As long as our knees are slightly bent we will not put strain on our lower back in this position. The shoulder blades are together in order to open the heart chakra but also to cause us to move from the shoulder blades rather than the shoulders. We are not lifting from the shoulders but pushing from the shoulder blades.

This area is the first area in a woman's body to suffer from Osteoporosis. It results in what is called the Dowager's Hump. The hump occurs because it is very difficult to work this area of the body. The Dance has given us the perfect cure—bat arms. On the metaphysical level this has bigger implications, which we will discuss later.

The wave originates in the heart chakra between our shoulder blades and moves through our arms and out through our fingers. This is often called snake arms in belly dancing because of the wave like movement. The snake is often associated with any wave like pattern because a snake obviously moves in a wave. In this Dance we want to make a distinction and not limit ourselves to the snake. All the movements are waves but take on very different qualities. We need to be more precise and look a bit deeper. Here we will focus on the bat or bird in relation to the arms. The direction of this wave is up and down.

Fish: The third movement is called the fish and is related to the element of water. In this case the wave also moves from foot to head through the body. The difference between the fish and the snake is the plane that the wave is moving through. The fish moves from front to back, where the snake moves from side to side.

If we look at the anatomy of the fish we see why we have two movements, one called the fish and one called the snake, rather than two snakes in different directions. The orientation in space is important so we will make the distinction from the very beginning.

Imagine the human skeleton, our spinal column with ribs protruding out on both sides, and our head on top. Our eyes face front perpendicular to our ribs. When we visualize the snake we see that it has a similar orientation. So when it undulates the movement is side to side in relation to its spinal column.

The fish is orientated differently. If we were to look at a fish, its spinal column runs through its body from head to tail but its bones or ribs run up and down rather than side to side. The fish undulates from side to side, but in relationship to it skeleton it is making a perpendicular motion. If we align our ribs with the fish's ribs and move perpendicular to our ribs we will be moving from front to back in space.

Energetically, moving from front to back is very different than moving from side to side, making these two very distinct movements. When we rock from side to side we are balancing. When we rock front to back we are moving to a higher energy state.

This movement begins by focusing on the pelvis and merely moving it forward and backward. It is not like a pelvis thrust in which we isolate the pelvis forward and backward holding the upper body. We want to involve the whole body like the fish does, not isolate one

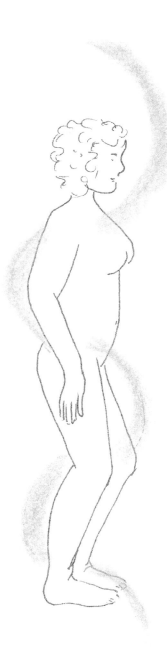

Fish Wave Movement

area. In the beginning you may feel that you are moving like a block, but just focus on the pelvic area. Originate the movement from there. After some time, when the body begins to relax, this movement will become very fluid and the wave will appear.

Lion: The last movement is the *shimmy* and relates to the earth element. The animal related to this movement is the lion. The earth element is sometimes thought of as the cow or bull but I think in this case the lion is more appropriate.

The shimmy is the most important movement in the Dance. Mainly because it is related directly to the earth element and on some level this is an Earth dance. We are using the Earth's energy. It is never as apparent as with the shimmy. During the shimmy the body vibrates at a very high frequency making it very different from the other movements. Where the other movements are obvious wave patterns the shimmy is a vibration. We are shaking things off and potentizing ourselves at the same time. The direction of wave is through.

This is where we need to think about amplitude and frequency. We begin the movement slowly making obvious waves but as we speed it up it becomes a vibration. We no longer see a wave movement but feel a vibration. This is why belly dancers wear scarves with coins or something metal that makes noise on them—so that you hear the movement. It is very fine and very subtle. This movement is meant to be felt or heard more than seen.

I recommend you don't begin with scarves that make noise. It will confuse you if you are off the beat. Once you are more familiar with the movement then use them. It will add a whole new dimension to what you are doing.

The movement itself originates from the knees; the bridge between the root chakra and earth chakra. The key to this movement is in the knees. It is *very* important to do this movement correctly.

The knees bend and straighten alternating from one leg to the other but always bending straight ahead, directly over the feet. Never let the knees roll in or move from side to side. They only move forward and backward, the way they were designed to move. The shimmy is instigated from the knees but the vibration occurs throughout the body. Generally the places where we have the most fat (liquid, water element) are the ones that will vibrate the most, like the hips and buttocks.

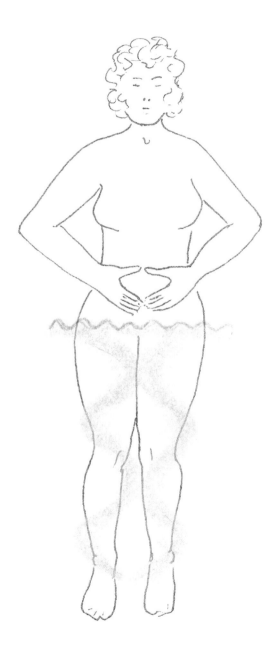

Lion Wave Movement

Waves move along a *medium*. In this case the medium is the body. Waves easily change direction following whatever medium they are moving along. This wave begins moving from the floor, front to back in the direction of the knees. It moves up from the knees until it hits the hip joints. The hips and pelvis are oriented from side to side, so when the wave hits the hips it reorients itself. As long as the hips are not locked the vibration moves easily along its new path across the pelvis. The more you bend your knees and relax the pelvis the more vibration you will generate.

The explanation seems very complicated, but the movement is very natural. And because the movement originates from rhythmically bending and straightening the knees (just like walking) it is simple and endless. It becomes a very monotonous movement, just like rocking, once you connect into it. When you have mastered the shimmy it becomes part of you. You will do it naturally without even thinking. You will begin to shimmy every time you hear drums.

Energy cannot flow through contracted muscles.

Traditionally shimmies are taught by contracting the muscles as a kind of spasmodic movement. Energy cannot flow through contracted muscles. Although this might look OK, it stops the flow of energy. If our aim is to move energy through our bodies then that is *not* a good way to do it, at least not for this Dance.

By using the knees we create perpetual motion. Once we get into the movement it can go on forever all we need to do is continue alternating the knees forward and back (never straightening the knees completely or locking them) as simply as if we were walking. When we learned to walk it was difficult in the beginning but later became a mindless movement. The shimmy will be the same.

Shimmies can be learned by following these simple steps. Stand in *wu chi*. Begin by bouncing up and down, both knees straightening and bending at the same time; very simple. Never let the knees straighten completely. Locking the knees stops the flow of energy. Be sure the knees are hip width apart; feet are straight-ahead, not turned out. As you bounce your knees go directly over your feet.

Just bounce in time to the music. Do this as long as you need to, until you are completely comfortable with the beat. Once you are connected to the beat, mindlessly bouncing—alternate the knees, one bent and one straight (never locked). Really use the knees. Allow them to bend, and release. Do not lock the hips. Keep everything soft. If the knees are bent and the hips are not locked the movement will naturally move out through the hips. Just allow your rear end to wiggle back and forth, but maintain proper posture.

Continue doing this movement until you are really comfortable with it. It will begin to loosen the body up. Then double time; do the movement twice as fast, the same movement, alternating knees—but remember amplitude and frequency. When we move faster (frequency) the amplitude (distance) has to be smaller.

Do the movement as fast or slow as you can. When you get lost go back to bouncing. Don't try to fix it—just start again. In time the shimmy will be as easy as just bouncing to the music. Trust me! It will happen. I can do shimmies talking, washing dishes, brushing my teeth... anything. This movement will become second nature and when it does you can move on, upward, outward, the sky's the limit. If I do nothing else in my life—I want to teach women to shimmy!

Once we have mastered each movement individually we can bring them back together in the Dance, rejoin them, like the dragon. This may be as far as you want to go at this point, mastery of the movements. We also have the choice of moving the movements up to the next level, integrating the energy and power of the High Priestess.

HIGH PRIESTESS

The High Priestess moves us from the physical realm into the spiritual realm. She is a "messenger of the gods" or in our case the goddess—as she connects us to the feminine aspects of the Divine.

Through her we explore higher vibrations of the elements we are already working with. The High Priestess is the catalyst, the bridge. This is why a magician or alchemist always has a female assistant—she is their catalyst. She provides the subtle realm, the *real* magic, that which is unseen, un-manifested but felt. She creates the shift that needs to occur between dimensions.

With her we begin working with intuition and guidance rather than control or manipulation. In relation to the Dance we move from tribal dance to sacred dance. We know the manifested aspects of the elements we are using; now we add the more subtle ones. The aspects we do not control but only intend or draw-in.

Adding intention to the Dance makes it truly sacred. While Dancing we can hold an over all intention such as the reason for doing the Dance, perhaps healing or celebration. At the same time we can also hold smaller essential intentions such as the wisdom behind each movement. This is how we work with the subtle realm.

Think of it as subtle vibrations as opposed to large waves. In doing this we can activate energy at the archetypal or universal level. We then add this to the physical level—the wave patterns we learned in the last chapter.

The High Priestess also represents the Sacred Prostitute archetype. The sacred prostitute like the "virgin" has reintegrated the two aspects of the serpent goddess—the sexual and spiritual. There is an excellent book on the importance of this archetype to our psyche today. It is called *The Sacred Prostitute* by Nancy Qualls-Corbett. I encourage any woman on a spiritual path to read it.

Nancy Qualls-Corbett writes:
"Like Adriane, the sacred prostitute is an archetypal image of one who has been initiated into the mysteries and achieved a profound connection with the goddess of love. Having integrated the goddess potency, she can then mediate the demands of the unconscious to other females when the safety of conventional structures is called into question.

The sacred prostitute is therefore that human woman who, through formal ritual or psychological development, has consciously come to know the spiritual side of her eroticism and lives this out according to her individual circumstances. We find her in all walks of life. One feels a certain *presence* in her midst, a combination of joy and wisdom. She is "one-in-herself", free of the confines of convention; she lives her life as she chooses.

Such a woman may not be considered sexy or provocative in the usual sense of these words, for her sexuality is not superficial, not motivated by conscious design or unconscious demands. It is not a learned behavior, an acquired skill or matter of ability, but rather a subtlety of her being springing from the depths of her soul. Her countenance holds a power, 'a mysterious power that everyone feels but that no philosopher has explained'" (Qualls-Corbett 1988, 74).

Isis was the High Priestess in Egyptian mythology. And since this is the manifestation of the archetype that I connected to I will talk about her here. There may be other manifestations from other mythology that resonates more deeply with you. If so just change the name to the one that resonates with you more.

Isis was strongly connected to Hat-hor, the Earth mother, the Empress archetype. Hat-hor means "house of *Horus*" or the "womb of the Hero". Where Hat-hor is Mother Earth the feminine energy, Isis is the human priestess that brings that energy in, brings it to Earth. She did this mainly through the sacred arts such as healing which included astrology, dream work and sacred dance.

Hat-hor's temple in Upper Egypt is called Dendera Temple. Behind the large temple is a smaller temple for Isis. The very famous astrological disk, which now resides in the Louvre, was originally from Dendera Temple. The disk is yet another expression of the archetypes, and full of wisdom.

Power Animals-Invoking the Energies of the Animals

When I introduced the movements I named them, like in tai chi, by the animal the movement imitates. This was to give you a simple idea of what the movement looks like. Animals tend to have very distinct movements. When we look at something that occurs in nature we remove the cultural boundaries and see things in a more basic or archetypal form. That was all we needed to know at that level but now we are moving up to a higher or subtler level.

Just as we can imitate animals we can also invoke the animal's power. *Power animals* are very common in all shamanic cultures. The Pharaohs (ancient Egyptians) were a shamanic culture. The *neteru* (plural for *neter/ntr*) were totems. By using totems we can *invoke* the energy of a particular animal.

We each have our own individual power animals. They come to us in many different ways, in dreams or in person, bringing us messages. My power animals are the spider, the bat and the snake.

The spider has come to me since childhood in dreams. Only once, recently, did I encounter a large tarantula in person. I'm sure I have encountered many spiders over my lifetime but none of them so dramatic that they caught my attention—until the tarantula. My feeling when I saw it was that this aspect, the wisdom of the spider, was beginning to manifest in the external world where before it had only been present on a subconscious level. What I had carried with me since childhood would now come into play in my life. This piece is still unfolding.

My experiences with the snake and bat were much more obvious. They came to show me something, to give me a message. From them I have learned a lot.

The snake's wisdom is transformation and healing—transmutation. The Ouroboros, the snake eating its tail, is a symbol from alchemy, the process of transmutation. The Caduceus (Hermes staff) is another symbol using the snake. In this case there are two snakes representing the sexual and spiritual energy. This symbol was originally used as a symbol of healing (the balancing of our energies) but later adopted by the medical and pharmaceutical communities.

I learned that in the Mayan astrology I am the *Snake*. This didn't surprise me at all. The snake in the Mayan astrology is all about fluidity, movement and creation. Even though I was not conscious of this until my mid-forties the energy had been vibrating within me to the point that I was attracting snakes into my life to open my awareness.

Two Serpents, Temple of Kom Ombo, Aswan, Egypt

My first encounter with the snake, a cobra, was many years ago, only a couple of years after arriving in Egypt. We were living in the countryside on an island in the Nile. We did this every summer during the mango season, which was the family business. My daughter was very small perhaps two years old. The house we lived in was an old stone house. I was walking down the hallway. As I passed by the doorway to one of the rooms, out of the corner of my eye I saw what looked like leaves blowing in the wind. "Hang on there are no leaves in the house!" I went back to the doorway and looked into the room to see what was blowing across the floor.

Just then time slowed down. It wasn't something blowing across the floor; it was a snake gliding across the floor. I stood mesmerized.

It was the most beautiful thing I have ever seen in my life. The way it moved was amazing. It was moving sideways across the floor as if it was hovering just above the surface. It was a stone floor, very uneven, but it seemed to cause no resistance for the snake. It moved as if it was floating.

I stood there watching, transfixed, as it made its way from one end of the room to the other. It undulated back and forth as it breezed across the floor. When it reached the wall it went straight up the wall and out through the chimney.

I wasn't afraid. I never thought for a moment that the snake would attack me. I just stood there frozen in time admiring the beauty of this creature not two feet in front of me.

When it left the room the spell was broken. I was back to reality and realized that there is a snake in the house! I was alone there with my two-year old daughter. Watching the snake was one thing; not knowing where it had gone was another. The experience was beautiful but not being a snake charmer and knowing nothing about snakes I felt it would not be safe to stay in the house with a cobra.

I ran out the back door to find *OmaToba*, the woman that helped around the house—to send her for help. I didn't know much Arabic at the time but I knew the word for "snake", *taaban*! She heard me and freaked out. She began running around like crazy screaming *"taaban, taaban!"* The office was nearby and she managed to panic over that way and get "help".

She returned with *Gidu Soliman* (Grandpa Soliman)—the only person she found in the office. Great! *Gidu Soliman* was about ninety years old and ninety percent blind. But came he did and with a big stick. He shuffled his way into the house and into the room where the snake had been spotted. He sat down, big stick in hand, and held vigil ready to strike, while *OmaToba* ran off screaming, looking for someone else to help us. I stood at the door of the room watching this brave old man protect me. I couldn't leave him alone. If the snake returned he would be right in its path and never see the snake coming.

Help arrived. The solution was to cement up the fireplace completely, so that the snake could not enter the house. Later that snake was seen running away over the top of the house. But the next day his mate was found. Apparently they always travel in pairs. I was also told that they *never* come in the house. I guess he must have been looking for me then—because somehow he ended up in the house.

The story spread quickly around the island, but in this version it was told that I killed the snake, probably with my bare hands! *Snake woman*. People looked at me differently after that day. They called me *Doctora* out of respect. All thanks to my power animal.

People feel the power of the snake and they fear it. I wasn't fearful when I was alone with the snake. It was only when I came back to *reality* that I felt there might be danger.

My second encounter with the cobra was in that same house. It seems that snakes don't actually know that they *never* go into houses. It was perhaps a year later, the summer of 1990. This time I was pregnant with my son.

I was 8 months pregnant. Bladder capacity was low. I was making a late night trip to the "bathroom". There was no electricity on the island so we had only candles and a flash light to light our way in the house. I didn't see the snake when I was going into the bathroom. He was to my right and the beam from the flashlight was straight ahead. It was only when leaving the bathroom that I saw him in front of me. As the light hit him he slithered off into the room behind him. I slithered off back to the bedroom to wake my husband.

My husband seemed uninterested that "there's a cobra in the house!" No way was I staying in a house, in the darkness, with only a flashlight and a cobra! We left in the middle of the night over the bumpy dirt road. I cradled my belly, hoping not to give birth on the way back to Cairo. When the others awoke in the morning and found the car missing they we sure I had given birth in the middle of the night. No, not so lucky, another cobra instead. They went into the house and found it still hiding in the room it had escaped to. It hadn't moved all night.

Having two encounters with a cobra was enough to convince me that I had better look more deeply into what the snake was trying to tell me. Snakes are about power and sexual energy. But for me I feel that these experiences were related directly to the Dance.

I will never forget my first encounter with the snake. The time I spent mesmerized, watching him, did something to me. I can see it as if it is happening right now. If nothing else I can truly connect to what I saw, how the snake moved. I didn't just watch that snake. I felt it moving. Each time I Dance and do the Snake, all I need to do is to connect back to that feeling and it moves through my body.

Not only do the animals contain this wisdom and power but I also believe that we can invoke these feelings or powers inherent in animals. Animals come to bring us messages, but we can also connect to them at will and tap into the power that they possess.

This is what the Pharaohs were doing with the *neteru*. If we are lacking in some area and need to tap into a specific energy we can do that through invoking the power animal or the archetype. It was said that these people were worshiping the *neteru* like gods. I don't feel this is accurate. I don't think they were that misguided. Worshipping gods is giving your power away to that god (which is different than surrendering to the Divine) but invoking the energy of that *neter* is empowering.

We can do the same thing in the Dance. We can add to the Dance by invoking the energy of the animal that we are imitating. This is basically what the shamans are doing when they imitate animals.

I have had many encounters with the Bat, another of my power animals. The ones that came into the house always came directly into my room. Here in Cairo I often have bats outside my window. They talk to me all night, although I am not conscious of what they are saying. My experiences with them lead me to integrate them in the Dance.

I have had enough experience with power animals to now be able to identify when they have a message for me. We encounter animals all the time but they usually go unnoticed. When they have a message for you, you will see them. If you don't they come back again and again until you receive the message.

I have also had profound experiences with bats in Luxor Temple. When they come I always take notice because the bat heralds some kind of initiation or transition. Bats use their radar to navigate. There appearance in your life often precedes an increase in psychic abilities. Generally the initiation means that you are moving into a time where you will need some skill that you had not yet developed. You may need your radar to navigate the darkness.

In relation to the Dance the bat is our intuition and the ability to move to higher levels. As we develop our radar we are better able to navigate, first in our sacred dance, later in the universal dance. We invoke the power of the bat when we want to move higher or deeper as we navigate the darkness.

What the Movements Feel Like

In the previous chapter when I presented the four primordial movements and described what they look like, I explained that they are waves moving in different direction, on different planes. I named them by the animal we are imitating when doing the movements. All of which was very external.

As we move into the archetype of the High Priestess we add another dimension. We move beyond what the movement looks like externally to what it feels like internally. The High Priestess brings us the gift of intuition and allows us to glimpse behind the veil. Like the bat she navigates the darkness. She creates a bridge from the unconscious and grounds it to Earth.

As well as exhibiting a movement externally we are invoking higher energies internally, or subtly. As I mentioned earlier, this is the point where the tribal, primal, dance becomes sacred. What makes the Dance sacred is the intention behind what we are doing. At this point we add or invoke the intention behind the movement.

A Deeper Level of the Four Primordial Movements

Snake: The snake represents the element of fire. Fire is inspiration and transformation. The snake brings the energy in. When we do the snake movement we are bringing energy in, healing and sexual energy are passing through our bodies.

The snake is about death and rebirth. I like to begin and end any Dance with the snake. It is a good way to balance our energy at the beginning of the Dance.

Fire is our inspiration. Feel the energy moving up your legs and into the womb, your creative center. Allow it to gestate there for a while before moving it up through your body. To end the Dance we can return to the snake going out the way we came in, completing the circle, like the Ouroboros.

Fire is also about purification. Another intention to hold while doing the snake is that of purification and transformation. Feel the snake energy moving up through your body transmuting and purifying the body's energy. You may also feel your sexual energy pushing up through your body. Feel the wave moving through you as if you are experiencing your body from the inside out. It is a *very* powerful movement.

Bat: The bat utilizes the element of air. Using our arms we fly. We navigate through space. The bat is about transition and moves us to higher energy levels, new dimensions. I mentioned in the description of the movement that the shoulder blades must be together in order to open the heart chakra. The bat moves everything up to a higher vibration, the vibration of love, by engaging the heart chakra. When using the Dance for healing this becomes a very important movement.

Energy comes into the body, moves up to the heart chakra where it is transmuted to love and then moved out through our arms. We use our arms to embrace, connect, and move the energy out of ourselves to others.

The bat is an initiator, meaning that it opens new doors for us when we are ready. It also fine-tunes our radar and in the case of the Dance the signal we are following is the music. When you want to move to a higher vibration, fly there using bat wings. Navigate through the music. At times during the Dance just stop and do bat arms. What generally happens is that the more you fly the more the rest of the body gets involved.

Never stop any movement in the body. This Dance is not about suppression or isolation. Let the energy flow wherever it wants to go. We instigate movements and then free them to move where they will. Focus on the lightness of air. Feel that you are riding the currents in the movement. Feel the freedom.

Fish: The fish's element is water. It is immersed in it and cannot live without it. Water represents the emotions. We are touching deeply into the emotions and the emotional body when we do the fish.

The fish is about floating and flowing. The easiest way to do this movement is while walking, either forward or backward, not standing still. Begin by simply walking in time to the music. Then let the body relax more and more. Allow the movement to become "sloppier", more fluid. Imagine yourself moving through water. There is a slight resistance when moving in water. The movements become heavier and smoother. They are not jerky or hard. If you ever have the opportunity to do this movement in water you will master it immediately because there is only one way to move in water, fluid.

When I first explained the movement I focused on the pelvis. The sacral chakra is related to the element of water. It is where we contain the primordial waters. Feel the movement originating from the womb and moving through the body.

After you have done the movement walking, try it standing in one place. Plant your feet on the floor and do the "mermaid". Your feet become the fins. Imagine you're a mermaid swimming through the water. What you will notice when doing the movement this way is that you *need* to work through your knees, ankles, and feet. This is an important exercise because it shows us how everything is connected and how the waves need to move. When we are walking the wave is moving out through the lifted foot. When we are stationary the wave still needs to move through the joints, even if they are not lifting off the floor.

Lion: The shimmy is the movement representing the earth element—the lion. This movement is about power, grounding and discharging energy. We bring this power up from the Earth through our knees to the root chakra and release it out through our hips. The vibration is released through our hips but the movement originates from the knees. It is connected to the root chakra more than the sacral chakra. It is raw feminine power.

It is best to Dance in bare feet. It helps us to feel the connection to the Earth. The feet are very important in this Dance and especially in this movement. The feet should be flat on the floor. Try to connect with the whole foot and keep that connection during the shimmies.

We bring energy in and discharge it out. Be sure to discharge the energy. If too much energy builds without discharging you may have an orgasm (release). To discharge the energy either feel the energy moving back down your legs or do little kicks, rhythmically, between beats. This can be used as a variation to the movement.

THE EMPRESS (subtle body)

The Empress is the Earth Mother. She is all about creation, creativity and birthing. The Emperor represents the physical Earth. The Empress represents the subtle body of the Earth, the dynamic part. She is very much related to the planet Venus, which is not surprising as Venus is considered like a subtle body to the planet Earth.

Just as the Earth has a subtle body, so do humans. Our subtle body is our energy body. It contains the *chakras* our energy centers. The word chakra means spinning wheel. These spinning wheels lay just over the major glands of our endocrine system.

Energy is funneled in and out of the chakras. The energy is then fed directly into the endocrine glands. The endocrine system is what regulates the hormones and all the major functions in the body. This is why energy healing is so effective. It works directly with the main regulatory function in the body—the endocrine system.

The *Kundalini*, the serpent energy that resides at the base of the spine, moves up through the chakras. There are two serpents, the *Ida* and the *Pingala*. In yet another manifestation of the alchemical process they separate and recombine. The points where they recombine are at the major chakras. Resolving one level, they again separate and move up to the next.

There are seven major chakras and many minor chakras. We will focus on the seven major chakras and two minor chakras. Each chakra has specific elements, planets, emotional issues, drives, even senses related to them. Different sources may give you slightly different information; use what feels correct to you.

The point here is to give you a basic understanding of the subtle body and chakra system so you can integrate it into the Dance, not to

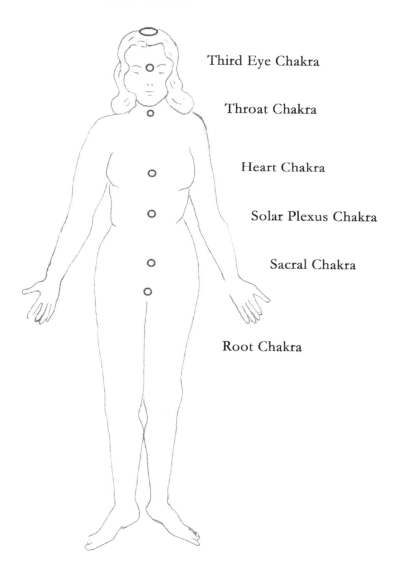

Crown Chakra

Third Eye Chakra

Throat Chakra

Heart Chakra

Solar Plexus Chakra

Sacral Chakra

Root Chakra

The Seven Major Chakras

fill you with information. There are many books written on the chakra system if you wish to deepen you knowledge in this area.

The Seven Major Chakras

Root Chakra: The root chakra is located over the perineum. It is related to the gonads in men and the 'G'-spot in women. It is the primal energy coming in to the system. It is often related to the emotion of fear. The root chakra opens downward. It is what connects us to the Earth. It can also be accessed through the knees.

Sacral Chakra: The sacral chakra lies over the womb. It is our creative center, our center of joy. It is connected to the ovaries. We Dance from the sacral chakra.

Solar Plexus Chakra: This is our ego center. The solar plexus is a point between our navel and the bottom of our ribs. It is connected to the liver. The issue it deals with is anger and is related to the element of fire.

Heart Chakra: The heart chakra is located in the center of the chest between the breasts. It lies over the thymus gland. It is our center of Love. It is the bridge between the lower chakras and upper chakras.

Throat Chakra: The throat chakra is our communication center. It is where we speak our will, our truth. It is related to the thyroid gland. This chakra is located at the base of the neck and opens to the back.

Third Eye Chakra: This chakra is located on the forehead, between the eyebrows, over the pineal gland. It is our psychic center. When we Dance we can use this center like radar and feel the music rather than hearing it.

Crown Chakra: The crown chakra is located on the top of the head, where our soft spot was as a child. It is what connects us to the universe. This chakra opens upward and is related to the pituitary gland.

Two Minor Chakras

Arch: This is where you will feel the pulsation of the Earth coming in and out of your body. Consciously connect from this place.

Palms: From here we consciously give out energy, connect with others whether it is hands-on-healing, stroking or holding hands.

In the Dance we are working mainly from the sacral chakra located over the womb. This is how the Dance became related to the belly. We move the energy up and down through our chakras. It collects, amplifies and transmutes in the vessel of our womb.

I have mentioned several times that this Dance is about relaxation. Allow the energy to move rather than *pushing* the energy. This principle is doubly important when working with the chakras. Kundalini work is not generally recommended for people under forty years of age. The body has not yet matured enough to handle the added energy. At about forty-one during our Uranus opposition the Kundalini energy begins to spontaneously move. Moving that energy prematurely can be dangerous.

I had some very sever Kundalini experiences in my late thirties. I was not consciously trying to move the energy, but the things that I was doing were making it move. The experiences were very painful. When I realized what was happening I was careful not to push the energy. After my Uranus opposition, these experiences of the energy rising were no longer painful. I would feel the energy moving but my body seemed able to deal with it. In order to avoid all of this it is best just to allow the energy to flow where it will, don't force it—just be conscious of it.

The Empress is also about creation, fertility and birthing. Now that we have learned the basics we can stop focusing on the specific movement and focus back on the Dance as a whole. We are ready to move to the creative phase. All the knowledge of the elements and of the Dance are within us—we have been seeded. Now we let the music guide us.

Music, like energy, moves in waves. The Earth is pulsating. We can tap into that pulse. It is rhythmic. When a musicians play a piece of music they are tapping into that pulse. The music itself, what we hear, is related to the Emperor, but its source, the pulsating subtle body of the Earth is related to the Empress.

In time you will feel the music. It will pass through you. In the beginning you are like the dragon—all the elements are joined together but still distinct. You dance one move after the other, bringing them all together in a Dance.

Different types of music *feel* different. Some movements just feel more comfortable with different sounds, rhythms or instruments. This differs from person to person, which is what makes the Dance individual and creative. Different instruments resonate in different parts of our body.

We usually feel drums in the hips, knees and rear-end; Earth. They work perfectly with shimmies. Lighter instruments, wind instruments, guitars, violins, make us feel the lightness of air. Fire and water might be more obvious in the rhythms than the instruments. Slow elongated sounds make us feel the fluidity of water. Sudden bursts make us feel volatile like fire.

We allow the music to be our guide. This is where the creative process really begins. We have done the ground work, now it is time to be creative and joyful. It is important to find music you like because it will inspire and move you.

Once you have broken down the music with the movements, identified themes and instruments, it is time to bring it together again. Generally a piece of music has several themes and instruments. Part of the creative process of the Dance is jumping from one to another. This is when we tap into the bat energy. Basically we are navigating, using our radar.

After navigation is fusion. The challenge of doing all the movements at the same time! Just as all the instruments play a piece of music together; we too can play it all together in our bodies. This is when we touch the Universal Dancer. As I mentioned earlier there are no limits. But don't expect to get it all at once. The journey is the path. It is the fun we have along the way, not struggling to get to the end that is important.

Dancing the Room

Generally when I Dance I stand in one place. I don't move much from my center. I like to ground, connect my roots, and then continue to funnel energy in. I felt that moving around the room a lot would diffuse the energy I had tapped into. Also the amount of energy coming through is immense and it often makes it difficult to move in space.

As I mentioned any piece of music has many elements, different rhythms and different instruments. One drum might keep the beat, another half timing, yet another double timing. It is pretty easy to find anything you want in a piece of music. Although I know everything is present in a piece of music certain things seem to jump out at me. That is what I follow.

One evening I was at my Studio, Dancing. I was using a piece of music that I had Danced to often. Even so, it is always a new experience. I was standing in the part of the room in which I usually stand. Not sure why I always stand in the same place. I suppose because of the way the speakers are positioned. For some reason I was inspired to change my place. It wasn't conscious. I just moved to another part of the room. I didn't even realize what had happened until I began feeling a very different energy emanating from the floor. I found this very curious. I Danced there for a bit and then I moved to another spot. Again I found the energy very different from where I had just been.

I continued doing this all the way around the room. Each position felt very different. Although I was letting the energy coming up from the floor guide me, I could still integrate that with the music I was hearing because somewhere in that piece of music was the same rhythm. When I found the rhythm then all the components were synchronized.

My feeling now is that often the things that are "jumping" out at me are probably the ones resonating with the other energy flowing around me. Although it is nice to Dance to music it is also possible to just pick up on the rhythm of the Earth and follow that.

I recently had the opportunity to see the New York City Ballet do a Jerome Robbins piece called *Moves*. It was very interesting because it is not danced to music. What I noticed was how responsive the dancers were to each other, as though there was something moving from one person to another. As if they were passing a baton to each other. I imagine what they were passing was control, or leadership, because at different points in the Dance different people had to be the catalyst to the next move.

What I saw in this piece, that I hadn't seen in any of the other ones, was flow. I could actually feel it moving from one person to another through the dance. In the other pieces all the dancers were following the music, which was following the conductor. I suppose when there is no music it becomes a collective or cooperative journey, without one leader.

THE EMPEROR (physical body)

The Emperor and the Empress are very closely connected. They both represent aspects of the Earth. Although one is subtle and one is manifested it is often difficult to separate them because of their deep connection. The one you are probably most familiar with is the masculine aspect which is why in our classes we spend a lot of time attuning ourselves to the feminine, the less familiar aspect.

I used the example of music to illustrate the two archetypes. The music we hear, the external sound, relates to the Emperor, the manifested. The pulse instigating the sound, the rhythm from the Earth, relates to the Empress.

At this stage we will focus a bit more on our music since it is an important component in the Dance. The type of music you use will depend on two things, the purpose of the Dance and what you like or what moves you emotionally.

I Dance to all kinds of music. A lot of it is Arabic music because it lends itself to the Dance. Good Arabic music will usually have drum riffs, which are fun to dance to. Any music with a heavy drumbeat will help because you will feel it strongly. I also use a lot of Celtic music and sometimes heavy metal, which often has a very tribal feel.

One of the first things I discovered in teaching dance is how many people cannot hear the beat. This seems to be quite common. Because of this it is a good idea to spend a lot of time just bouncing to the rhythm. Children do this naturally. If you cannot hear the beat it is probably because at some point in your life you were told to stop bouncing and sit still. It is time to start bouncing again!

I have spent many classes just walking in time to the music with students. If you are having trouble hearing the beat find music with a heavy drumbeat. Simply walk, clap or bounce until you begin to feel it. You will reconnect. It is just a matter of reprogramming the old programming that told you to be still.

At this point it might be a good idea to just spend some time with the music. In my classes I teach each movement one at a time. We do one movement for an entire song. Obviously we do this to become familiar with the movement by repeating it over and over again—until it becomes a natural part of us. But at the same time we are doing something else, we are exploring the variations of one movement through a whole piece of music with all its dynamics.

As a child I was told I had "ants in my pants". I could never sit still. Try as they might my parents never succeeded in making me sit still. There was no way I was going to stop moving. What I have discovered as an adult is that if I am not moving—I cannot feel my body. Those visualization that have us lie down and then ask us to feel our foot, our hand—I cannot. If it is not moving it doesn't exist, or perhaps I cannot quantify it. Movement is so intrinsically woven into my being that when I am not moving I literally feel I am dead.

Music also gives us the sense of community because it allows us to Dance together in a group. Dancing in a group is an amazing experience. If you don't have a group of women you Dance with, find one, or make one. The energy builds when you Dance in a group.

We also use the principle of *entrainment* in a group. Entrainment is when a group is resonating or pulsating together. It is why women living together begin to menstruate together, or clocks in a shop begin to tick together. It is also what happens between mother and child when their hearts begin to beat together. We can use entrainment consciously to assist each other in the movements. In my classes if someone is having trouble finding the movement I ask her to just focus on my body. In sort of a meditative state she can connect with me and my movements—if her mind relaxes and focuses outward, it frees her from control and she will begin to move with me.

When I began explaining the Emperor I mentioned how closely related the subtle body is to the physical body, how they influence each other making it difficult to speak about them separately.

Just as the rhythm creates the blueprint for the sound, or the beat, our subtle body creates the blueprint for how we manifest in the physical word. The body we have grown into is a manifestation of who we are internally. Our body type defines who we are. Because of this deep interrelatedness it is also easy to see the issues we are dealing with based on how our body has manifested.

Through the Dance we can learn to embrace our bodies. As we release and surrender to the Dance, we find our bodies changing. What better way to manifest the perfect body than to use it, perfectly. We can either work from the inside out or the outside in.

Each body part has a metaphysical component. We have the physical level; how we use that body part and then we have the higher meaning, what that means on the emotional or metaphysical level. It is possible to read the body just by looking at it.

All of our lessons, dysfunctions, and attributes show in the body. Our body type defines an inner, deeper; meaning of ourselves and it is manifested physically. This is why it is best to work with the body, try to heal it rather than just trying to force a change by plastic surgery or other drastic means. Our physical body is giving us a clue as to what we need to work through in this lifetime. Work through it on the emotional and spiritual level and it will change on the physical level.

Wilhelm Reich and Alexander Lowen did a lot of work on this subject. There is also a lovely book *Eastern Body, Western Mind* by Anodea Judith that can take you deeper into his subject. Most of us have had our body type since birth, just as we have had our temperament. These define deep, life path, issues so work with them rather than trying to ignore or deny them.

Really take a look at your body. Don't be afraid. Any part of your body that you feel is especially beautiful will define where you have an abundance of healing energy, and where you shine. Of course often our definition of beauty is skewed due to cultural definitions but try to get beyond that and really *see* yourself. All my life I was told that I had beautiful hands, not surprising that I went on to do hands-on-healing. I also use my hands to transmit and initiate, and write!

More transient issues, or the effects of not resolving the deeper issues, will result in *dis-ease*. We can read the deeper issues depending on where the dis-ease is manifesting the body. The body is speaking to us.

Being conscious of the body and how it speaks to us, adds yet another layer to the Dance. This works in two ways. The first is by making our movements or intentions more conscious. If we know what the body is saying we can use it to move the Dance, or our intention, in that direction. For example if we are Dancing for grounding, or to discharge energy, and we know that it is the feet that create our connection to the Earth, then we can be sure to emphasize this aspect during the Dance. We would make sure that our feet remain on the ground during the Dance. We could also kick to discharge; perhaps even stamp our feet on the floor.

The second aspect is that of using the body to feed back to us. When you are learning the movements notice where problems arise. Which movements are difficult for you? What part of the body is stiff or not responding? This can give you great insight as to where your blockages are. For example there are some people who **cannot** keep their feet on the floor. When they do shimmies their heels always come off the floor. These people are probably not well grounded.

The most common problem is stiffness in the pelvic area. Generally this is related to holding or repression. It could be repressing joy, a fear of moving forward, or a repression of sexual feelings. Or it could be cultural programming that causes us to deny this part of our body.

In time the movements become easier. Where we are holding, or blocking, usually reaches a threshold and releases. Watch the process unfold. As you free yourself emotionally you will free yourself physically. Your body will actually change shape and at the same time you will begin to embrace parts of your body that you previously rejected because they did not fit into your ideal picture of yourself. My body changed a lot from the Dance. I feel it has been sculpted by the Dance. I never truly embraced my hips and buttocks before. Now I understand what they are really for!

Below I have given a brief description of each body part that we will use in the Dance and the metaphysical significance. For a deeper understanding on this subject see *You Can Heal Your Life* by Louise Hay or *The BodyMind Workbook* by Debbie Shapiro.

The Body Speaks

Feet: The feet are what ground us to the floor. They are our connection to the Earth. They create stability for us, allow us to walk and move forward. They are very sensitive to the Earth, acting like a bridge. All of our nerve endings end up in the feet making them a mirror of the whole body (the premise behind reflexology). It is best to Dance in bare feet in order to make a strong connection to the Earth. This will also help you with proper positioning. During the Dance be sure to use the feet as much as possible. Really work through them. Do not exclude them from the Dance.

Pelvis: The pelvis houses our sacral chakra and our womb. It is our center of creation and birthing. This is most often where women are *holding* and have a lot of locked energy. This may come from sexual repression or promiscuity—either way we are cutting off this part of ourselves. This Dance is the perfect vehicle for releasing this energy and reconnecting with our sacred sexual, creative selves. For women this area is also our center of gravity.

Buttocks: This is one of the main areas where we hold tension, and usually don't realize it. It is where we sit so we need to take this into consideration. Because it is linked to the root chakra it is where our power resides and is initiated from. It is actually the buttocks that move the pelvis forward. When we are holding ourselves, which usually means repressing something, we are generally clenching the buttocks. While Dancing, especially in the shimmies, try to relax this part of the body as much as possible.

Waist: The waist divides the body in two parts, the upper half and the lower half. In the beginning there is usually stiffness here. It is not an area of the body that we move much. After time this will loosen. It is important to move through the waist. We tend to be able to move either the top part of our body or the bottom. Because the movements are waves and this is a full body experience, we need to learn to move through the waist. We need to bridge the upper and lower spheres.

Chest/Breasts: The chest houses our heart. The heart chakra resides just between our breasts. The breasts are one of the greatest symbols of femininity. With our breast we nourish. It is no wonder that the heart chakra is nestled between them. As we nourish our loved ones from our breasts, they are imbued with our heart chakra energy. Movements engaging the chest or breasts are moving that energy outward.

Arms: We use our arms to embrace. The heart chakra energy moves from the chest out through our arms and through our hands and fingers. Arms help us balance. They involve a lot of moving and lifting. Whether we are lifting others or lifting ourselves the arms lift us up.

Shoulders: The shoulders are where we carry our burdens. We carry the weight of our head, our thinking and mental processes, on our shoulders. In this Dance when we move the arms we are careful to move them from our shoulder blades (wing bones) not from our shoulders. The reason being that we do not want to include our burdens in the Dance. It makes us heavy. We want to fly using the heart chakra energy available through the shoulder blades.

In the Dance we use our shoulders in a very different way, to instigate movement. We can use the shoulders to do shoulder rolls, which are very slow and seductive. We also use the shoulders to initiate breast shimmies. In this case the shoulder begins the movement and momentum takes over. In both of these movements the shoulders move forward and backward, which is releasing, rather than up and down which would create more stress and strain.

Soft Tissue

Something else I would like to mention that is not a body part, but that is part of our body, is fat. Western culture has a negative obsession with fat. Before we reject it perhaps it is best to first understand it. Fat is used for many reasons. There are metaphysical aspects to it as well. It doesn't just come from gluttony or over-eating.

We know that fat works as an insulator. We are perfectly willing to accept that fact when we are speaking about polar bears and acknowledge that they wouldn't survive without it! Neither would we. Just as the polar bear uses fat for protection, so do humans. In our case it is not against the freezing cold weather or some other harsh physical environment like the polar bear but a harsh emotional environment.

We build fat to protect ourselves emotionally. Before you go and have liposuction take note of *where* your body is accumulating fat. Where does your body feel it needs to be protected? That is how you will know what you are protecting. My guess is that if you just go ahead and remove the fat by surgical means, you will leave your body feeling vulnerable. The body will then seek out other means of protecting itself.

Fat is also used as an insulator in another way. Just as we use plastic to insulate wires, our body uses fat to insulate our meridians. When I began doing energy work, especially healing, I gained a lot of fat. It seemed to suddenly appear for no apparent reason. At one point I lost quite a bit of it and found that after healing treatments I felt like I had been plugged into an electrical socket.

Some wise soul appeared in my life at that point in time (can't even remember who it was). He told me that this was common and that the fat is the way the meridians have of protecting your energy system. I don't think this is necessarily true for everyone (that you will gain weight if you do energy work). Personally I know I have electrical issues. I tend to freeze my computer and blow up lights when I get angry. I can't wear watches because I stop them. Perhaps I am an extreme case but it is good to take this into account when you are looking at your body and wondering—why?! It may be a gift not a curse.

Fat is also a survival mechanism. We accumulate it from a sense of scarcity. The more you starve yourself the more your body tries to build fat. It is a self-preservation reaction. The body has a wisdom all its own. If you want to change something it would be best to work with it instead of against it. You will find that your body is a whole lot smarter than you are. It has preserved our species for millions of years!

Cellulite, on the other hand, is a bit different than fat. When we are examining where we have fat we also need to consider what kind (the body is full of clues to our healing). Cellulite is water (emotions) and toxins in a latticework of fat. "Ah, the complicated webs we weave." In this case we are holding toxic emotions that need to be releases. Again, I suggest you do that in a healing way rather than an invasive one.

If all of this seems complicated and overwhelming remember that the Dance is a healing tool. Our body is speaking to us but if we can't hear it, for whatever reason, we will still move to healing just by doing the Dance. So it is a win/win situation. My experience is that once we begin to heal we gain more and more awareness. Once some of the layers are removed the process picks up speed. We get lighter. We begin to know what to do. To see clearly what needs to be changed and what needs to be embraced.

THE HIEROPHANT

The Hierophant prepares us for the last stage of this alchemical process, the dream of the sacred marriage. Up to this point we have learned the subtle and manifested properties of the elements we are using, as well as how to integrate the external aspects such as Earth pulse and music.

The Hierophant defines the form or the process we are using. He is a scholar, the High Priest. He is well versed in the sacred writings. He gives things form, definition, or the confirmation we seek to be fully conscious of our *knowing*. He gives order and understanding to our experience, allowing us to transmute, by truly integrating all of what we have experienced. He shows us Divine order, wisdom in form, through the language of alchemy.

Although the Magician is often called the Alchemist, the Hierophant is a higher vibration of this principle. Rather than acting out the practice the Hierophant holds the energy of the process. He is not connected to any one aspect but the universality of the process.

The operation that the Hierophant represents in the alchemical process is that of fermentation. Although I decided in the writing of this book that I would not speak about each operation of the alchemical process, I think the concept of fermentation is the best way to describe the function of the Hierophant.

What is different here, than from the manipulations of the Magician, is that we have moved to a higher energy level. The Hierophant takes us, with his sacred knowledge, into the spiritual realm. He is more a witness to the Divine than a manipulator. We initiate a procedure and then surrender to the Divine order. We bring the elements together and then allow them to ferment, create a new order. All the constituents are present, percolating, working together.

Manifestation

In essence, what distinguishes the physical from the emotion and spiritual is the frequency of the vibration. We know this from basic physics. In order for something to manifest, be physical, it needs to vibrate at a low frequency. The higher the frequency the lighter the vibration, the less "physical" and more etheric it becomes. Conversely higher frequencies can be brought into manifestation by slowing them down.

We know that water in the form of steam is very hot, therefore the molecules are moving very quickly. As we cool the steam, slow it down, it begins to get heavier until it becomes a liquid. If we continue to slow it down it will become a solid, ice.

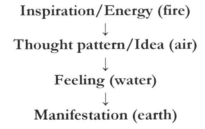

Inspiration/Energy (fire)
↓
Thought pattern/Idea (air)
↓
Feeling (water)
↓
Manifestation (earth)

Like in our example with water, most procedures can move in both directions. We can either slow down or speed up the vibration. There are many operations that seem to only move in one direction but at this level that is not true—anything is possible.

Sacred Geometry

As well as being well versed in alchemy the Hierophant holds the knowledge of sacred geometry. Music itself is a form of sacred geometry. The Pythagoreans were well known for their use of music. Rudolf Steiner also used music as a method for teaching mathematics. This method is still used in the Waldorf schools today.

Music is Divine order in form. Even if we do not read or understand music we can feel the rhythm, harmony, and sacredness of what is behind it. Sound healing is based on this principle. We can use tuning forks, crystal bowls, or the voice to produce sounds that are healing. As well as the vibration produced through sound there are also the more visual forms of sacred geometry such as primordial shapes.

Phi Φ, the twenty-first letter of the Greek alphabet, is a ratio that is thought to represent Divine unfolding itself. It represents the *golden section*, *golden mean* or *divine proportion*. This proportion is thought to represent the natural order. It is a proportion that nature naturally falls into. The Great Masters used this proportion in their paintings. A woman whose face exhibits these proportions is thought to be intrinsically beautiful. The ancient temples were built using these proportions.

Proportions were used rather than numbers because within a proportion there is movement. Numbers are static, too fixed, or concrete. Proportions show relationships and are dynamic. We are vibrating in a constant state of motion and change—not fixed like numbers. Fibonacci's sequence, often called the *matrix of creation*, is a variation of Phi. It produces a spiral. This spiral is found in nature in such things as shells and DNA.

When it comes to the Dance we can incorporate sacred geometry consciously. That is the role of the Hierophant in our Dance. Where the High Priestess intuitively connected us to the Divine order, the Hierophant does it consciously using sacred knowledge to raise the vibration.

We can Dance sacred geometry, either in relation to other people, our space, or within our own bodies. When Dancing with other people we can produce shapes, such as creating a spiral, Dancing in a circle, as well as moving energy between the other members of the group.

When preparing a sacred space we can use sacred geometry to clear the space. We can use symbols or sound. Members of the group can intone or chant. Flower remedies carry a vibration, we can use them to help create a sacred space and shift the energy.

Many of the movements automatically produce Divine shapes in our bodies. The snake easily falls into the infinity (∞) symbol, a continuous never ending circle, moving out and coming back. We can move the infinity symbol through our bodies with the snake or produce the symbol around us using this movement.

The best way to access information about sacred geometry is to first look for symbols or shapes that attract you. You can then look them up in a book on sacred geometry to determine their standard meaning. Or try to access the information yourself by sitting and meditating with the symbol. This is the best way to see what it means to you personally.

The Hierophant was the archetype that I resonated with the most throughout my life. Always seeing the Divine, I wanted to understand it. I clearly remember hearing "there is order in the universe, all man has to do is understand it". I must have been about nine when this happened. I can still relive the moment, as if it is happening now. It was a door opening and I was curious enough to go through.

As a teenager I was fascinated with magic and the occult. I would write papers for school about witchcraft, acupuncture, and other subjects that I'm sure shocked my teachers back in the 1970's. They must have thought I was insane but these were the things I was interested in and willing to write about.

At university I studied science thinking it would give me insight into this Divine order. That only took me to the point of the Magician because scientists often reject the Divine or things they can't control. So we only got as far as what could be controlled.

After my frustration with science and four years of biochemistry! I began to pursue psychology, philosophy, and religion. There was even a point where I considered becoming a nun to access this Divine realm. It was only when I came to Egypt that I encountered the concepts of *surrender* and *flow*. This was the piece that was missing.

I needed to break the cultural trance; leave Western society and their need for control to see that we don't need to control. Everything does move in Divine rhythm whether we try to control it or not. Control is an illusion. It is merely an ego state and has no place in the *natural* world. It's a good way to waste a lot of energy. When we flow we work with Divine order and build energy.

Once that veil was lifted my life was different. It took the energy of the High Priestess, glimpsing behind the veil, for me to truly be able to integrate all the wisdom of the Hierophant. To finally be able to use all the knowledge that I had been accumulating over the years.

Growing up in Western culture I had already connected to the masculine archetype of the Hierophant. It was the feminine aspect, the High Priestess, which I needed to integrate to be complete. For me this happened through the unfolding of the Dance. Once I was able to integrate the feminine aspect then both archetypes became fully available to me.

THE LOVERS

The Lovers embody the subtle aspect of the sacred marriage. It is the dream of the sacred marriage. It creates the desire for fusion. The dream is a virtual experience of fusion. It creates the passion or fire necessary to move us forward. It may come with information, or guidance, creating a yearning. It is usually at this point in our lives during the sacred marriage, around the age of forty-one, that we find our true calling. This is because when we have integrated the two sides of ourselves, we become whole and are empowered. It is the point where the Divine seeds that were planted from birth can come to fruition.

The Lovers card in the tarot is usually depicted as a man trying to make a choice between two women. The real message of this card is that of surrender—following Divine guidance or following our path. The masculine aspect is ready to combine with the feminine. It looks as though he has to make a choice between two paths (two women) but this is not the case. There is an angel, Cupid, with a bow and arrow. Cupid in fact is a messenger and will shoot one of the feminine aspects (possibilities) and remove it from his path. Divine intervention. Which aspect is removed will be based on where the man (masculine) is standing in purity and integrity, or which lesson he needs to learn next.

At this point in the Dance we focus on our intention as well as trying to hear that Divine guidance to help us find our way—the voice that will *lead* us through the Dance. We always navigate by the horizon; our intention is the point on the horizon that we are moving towards. The actual step-by-step path will unfold as we go along. We must surrender to that, always knowing that it is taking us where we need to go.

We can't always see the bigger picture but we can make a conscious intention as to where we would like to go. For example, if we were driving across the United States, say from New York City to San Francisco, we could use a map of the USA and choose what looks like the best route.

San Francisco is west of New York City that is the horizon that we are navigating towards. But we use the map to delineate each step we take. At times the road we are on may seem to be heading north, south, or even east! But then we find a huge mountain or canyon in front of us bringing sense to the change in direction. And even though we have had a slight wobble off what would appear to be the direct route west, we understand the wisdom in the deviation.

My experience of this aspect was literally a dream. It was at this point that I met my *twin flame*, my masculine side. He first appeared as my husband in a dream. It was a very powerful and prophetic dream. I didn't pay much attention to the messages. A hot guy and we were doing amazing things, what more could you ask for in a dream? But then he kept coming to me in different ways. He turned out to be a real man but not someone I had yet met in person.

Then one day in front of my face, I found his astrological chart— just by "chance". That is when I began to realize that there was a bit more to this than just a nice dream. I don't look at charts of people unless they ask me to. I feel it is an invasion of privacy. But this one was just there in front of me! I felt it was a gift that contained something I needed to see.

Needless to say he was also a Virgo and his chart was much like mine. I began to realize that I needed to look more closely at this. What qualities did this person have that I needed? Or that were mine and I wasn't seeing? This led me on another journey.

Suddenly Virgo males began appearing in my life when I hadn't known any before. I started looking at them and what they had to show me. One of them was an astrologer and I asked him about the chart I had found and what he felt about these similar aspects. He is the one that directed me back to the actual dreams. He told me to look more closely at what was going on there. He felt that was where the real information was to be found.

Luckily I had written many of the dreams down. Other ones impacted me so strongly that I can still relive them, which is also unusual. One of the dreams was a ceremony or ritual. I awoke crying from the emotional pain of the dream. At the time it made no sense but now I understand it and will integrate it into the higher levels of the Dance.

My twin flame began appearing outside of my dreams. I could *sense* him even when I was awake. The most interesting thing was how other people were seeing me. Everyone started asking me if I was having an affair! They told me I was glowing.

Then came the day that reality hit and I had to ask myself that same question, what was I doing? It is easy to justify connecting to someone else when they are not in physical form. But it was true I was somehow out of integrity with my marriage. I was in love with someone else, even if he was a part of me.

I consciously decided to end this "relationship" with my twin flame. I stopped pursuing this path and allowing him in. I have to say that it was one of the most difficult and painful decisions I have ever made in my life. And now, in retrospect, I can see how much I have learned from trying to do the "right" thing and not following my inner voice. It caused me great pain at the time. That should have been a red flag as to the importance of that decision. This was a part of me that I let go of for the sake of my marriage.

The Divine had other plans for me. I made a choice that apparently was not mine to make. Two years later I was divorced. It was my real life husband that Cupid removed from my path in, I might add, the most Divine way. The universe has a way of correcting itself. Just watching destiny unfold is an amazing process, so far beyond anything we could think of. But that's another story...

Intention is the direction we are moving. In the case of the Dance it is usually the type of energy we would like to bring in or the purpose of the Dance. But be willing to change direction at any time. Our intention may be simply to have fun or connect to the Earth. Or it may have a higher purpose, healing others, or ourselves, purification, or balance. In the Dance you will be moving lots of energy. For this reason it is important to have a good intention, a way to direct that energy. Surrender is also a good intention, or giving it up to the Divine and just seeing where that takes you.

Something that might not be considered a good intention is doing the Dance just to attract attention. If your desire is to take other peoples energy, then note that there must be a large energy deficit on your side. Taking energy from others is a very dangerous game. There are many kinds of energy and you won't know exactly what kind you are pulling in. When we move the Earth's energy through us we know what the source is. It is pure, free of its own intentions. To begin with limit yourself to working with the Earth and nature. As you progress and balance you will stabilize and things will become clearer. Working with others is something we will discuss in the last part of this book.

There are many types of *guidance*. The main similarity is that they free you from control. There is Divine guidance that might come into play when using the Dance for healing. The music itself is another guide that we will follow.

The first type of guidance that I present in my workshops is an initiation in the form of a guided visualization. It is an easy way to ease into the Dance without having to be conscious or in control. In the workshop we do the visualization early on, before the women learn most of the information you have already read. I hope this is a book that you will not just read once but work with. Read it all the way through to get the bigger picture and then go back and work with the details.

Although I hold the intention of an initiation in the reading of this book it is a good idea for you to make a conscious intention for yourself. You can take yourself through a similar process, initiating yourself. The intention here is to relax the body to make it receptive to the beat of the Earth. Attune yourself to the rhythm or pulsations emanating from the Earth. Use some kind of music with a heavy drumbeat. Then try to connect to the Earth's rhythm, to your own chakras, to the subtle energy as well as to the music.

Find a quite, sacred, space to work, a place where you will not be disturbed. Close the doors and curtains, and unplug the phone. You are creating a *womb* for yourself to birth out of. The whole process takes about 20-30 minutes. You may want to record a guided visualization on a tape so that you can completely surrender to the process.

You want to connect with the floor as much as possible. Stand in the *wu chi* position allowing the attunement to build potential. Use music that is slow and relaxing, but that has a rhythmic, heavy, drumbeat. This music will induce a trance state as well as allowing you to have the experience of connecting to the drum. Put on the music and position yourself. Take a couple of deep breathes, relax and begin the visualization.

Your visualization should include seeing yourself connected to the Earth and feeling the pulsation of the Earth. Feel the energy moving through your body and discharging negativity or toxic emotions. You may want to work through each chakra or do a progressive relaxation through each part of the body. Think about what it is that you intend to do during the visualization or what you want to achieve and then find the best way to get to that point.

THE CHARIOT

The Chariot is all about power and control. It is about *consciously* balancing our lives. In the tarot we see it as a charioteer trying to control his horses (spirit). It is the conscious aspect of the Dance. How we use and balance our own power. Where we direct our passion or how we let it flow.

When I speak of passion I mean the sacred fire that burns inside of us. This fire burns pure if you release it from ego. At this point in the process it is time to be humbled and release ego so that your manifestation becomes a reflection of Divine will. This is co-creation.

For me personally I was divorced and integrating both sides of myself. I was free to pursue my passion, the Dance, uninhibited. Looking back on it I can see that it needed to be this way. I needed to return to being the *Virgin* (the woman that is complete in herself, full of potential) to continue on my path. My husband was not the father of what I would birth next, so I could no longer be with him. It was for me to take control of both aspects of myself by surrendering to the greater process.

Ego is like contracted muscles. It will stop the flow of Divine energy. Ego is finite. This whole Dance is an analogy for the process of surrender and the amazing things we can achieve by doing so.

We can tone our muscles. We can work as hard as we can to do movements through building strength. Lifting our legs over our heads, jumping, controlling—or we can surrender. We can allow the unlimited energy to move through us. This ultimately leads us to more power than we could ever achieve on our own. The choice is yours.

You have learned all the elements individually. You feel the call or pull in a certain direction. You have an intention. You can take your own personal power and strength and move it with force (strong intention) in that direction.

What follows is what I take my students through in the workshop. I will give you an introduction, present some principles, suggest a warm-up and then a way to move through each movement.

Keep in Mind...

Before you begin to Dance there are some basic guidelines/principles to keep in mind. This Dance is very simple, in fact so simple that you will find it difficult in the beginning. The reason it may seem difficult is because these are very natural movements but we have been taught to move in very unnatural ways. So the first principle is: **Don't get frustrated**.

It will take the body time to undo all the bad programming that it has learned over time. This Dance is about relaxation. The more frustrated you become the more the body will become tense and ridged. This would be counter productive. The second principle is **relax**. Egyptian women, Middle Eastern women and women from tribal cultures have been dancing since they could stand. These movements are very natural to them.

We (in Western culture) have been taught to stop the movement in our bodies. We do this by holding ourselves—controlling our bodies. It takes time to relax and reprogram, be patient. Generally it will come in an instant, like a release. It is as if there is a threshold where the body "gets it". Suddenly it releases and you won't remember why you couldn't do this from the beginning. It is so easy and natural. It usually happens as an *ah-ha!* moment. Just create the space for that moment to arrive.

Whenever you can't *do* a movement, *visualize* it. You will be retraining the brain whether the body is actually responding or not. In time the body will catch up to the vision and that will be the ah-ha moment.

Avoid using mirrors. This Dance is about how it *feels*, not how it looks. It is internal, not external. No one can tell you that you are not doing the movement correctly. If you are connected into the movement, it is right. How you do the movement will be different for each person. Do not become the observer but the participant.

The only thing that is *wrong* is to be off center. This will hurt the body. Knees are always slightly bent. Never extend farther than you can go. This will throw you off your center. Feet should be straight not turned out, and knees always bend directly over your feet. They never wobble from side to side.

The position I described earlier is *wu chi*. It is a very natural position. And like in martial arts you never extent so far that you throw yourself out of alignment. Always be *over yourself* (aligned)—not too far extended. Apply the principles used in martial arts for staying centered and you will be in perfect alignment. Try to learn all the movements from this position. It may seem awkward in the beginning but it will become very natural.

Points To Remember:
- Don't get frustrated
- Relax-relax-relax!
- Visualize it
- Feel it
- Stay aligned

Warm-up

Before dancing it is always a good idea to warm-up. This is not a strenuous dance. You will loosen up while dancing but it doesn't hurt to warm-up or relax the body a bit. If you are not going to do a structured warm-up then just begin slowly and work up to really letting go.

I suggest you put on some peppy music. Move rhythmically increasing the movement as you go, just to bring up your heart rate and warm the body. Then stop with feet planted in *wu chi* loosen each part of your body in turn. Rotate the head and neck both directions, front, back, and side to side.

Then move down to the next section, the shoulders. Lift and drop the shoulders. Get the feeling of initiating a movement and then relaxing into it. Lift the shoulders and then just let them drop. Do the same by pushing the shoulder forward and then letting it fall back in place. Do both sides—several repetitions. Move on to shoulder rolls. Be sure to allow the shoulder blades to come together in the back, then up and over. Do shoulder rolls in both directions, back to front,

front to back. Be sure the knees remain slightly bent and the feet in *wu chi*.

Move on to the waist. Rotate the hips in a large circle. Balance and counter balance, meaning if the hips are forward the upper body is back and vice versa—spinning like a top. This is an easy movement and should feel more like leaning than making an actual movement.

Realign yourself in *wu chi*. Allow one heel to come off the floor. Work the hip by lifting and dropping. Initiate the movement and let it go. Change sides.

Warm up the knees by making small circles with the knees, one and then the other. Make a small circle, front, side, back, side. Be sure to work through the ankles and feet. We use the ankles and feet more than we are aware of, not so much in making actual movements with them, but in moving through them. When they are warm and loose they cause less resistance to the movement.

Position

It is best to Dance barefoot. We want to really feel the floor, so that we can connect with the Earth. Always begin the Dance with good posture, meaning starting in the *wu chi* position. Begin any dance by *marking time*—meaning feel the rhythm, get into the beat. The easiest way to do this is just to sway in time to the music. Remember the Dance is a process. We begin slowly and build. Most music works on the same principle. Don't give it all away in the beginning—work up to it.

Intention

While you are marking time or centering yourself set your intention if you have one. This part at the beginning of the Dance sets the stage for the rest. In fact this is when we are connecting to the primordial waters. Get in touch with your womb, your creative center. We create the primordial waters. Out of this we birth the Dance. In mythology the primordial waters were created and out of it emerged the serpent, the goddess Ishtar. She moves like the snake, that primal inspirational energy.

In alignment with this primordial blueprint, a good way to begin the Dance is to bring in the energy with the snake movement. Feel yourself bringing in the energy of the snake, pulling the waves up from the Earth through your feet. Continue this until you feel well centered, and you have prepared yourself, your intention and your focus. At that point there is usually a shift in the music. Music is generally written with these same principles/patterns so it is not difficult for it all to synchronize in intention as well as voice.

In the class we go through each movement, each element. We begin with fire then air, water, and earth. We do each movement to an entire song. Repetition is important especially since relaxation is paramount. By doing the movement repetitively we gain confidence and ease into a more relaxed state. Later in the class we bring all the movements together in the Dance. This is yet another example of the separation-recombination process.

Let's Dance!

Begin with the **Warm-up** and then just flow into the **Movements** from there.

We begin the movements with **Fire**, the **Snake**. Start by just swaying to the music allowing the body to get looser and looser. Shift your weight from one side to the other, just marking time (getting into the beat of the music). It is *very* important that you hear the beat because this is what aligns you with the pulse of the Earth.

If you are having trouble hearing the beat then just spend some time with this, just sway or clap out the beat. If you relax enough and focus on the beat you will eventually move into the rhythm. This is called entrainment. Things in close proximity will synchronize, just allow it to happen.

Once you are well connected to the beat let your movements become bigger as your body relaxes more and more. At this point we are only working on one plane, from side to side, as if there was a piece of paper cutting through our body separating back from front. On this piece of paper we could draw a wave pattern from foot to head. That would be the wave that we are following.

Now try to bring the movement up through your body rather than letting it be lost from side to side. This will intensify the movement. Focus on brining the movement up to your hips. Now we are focused on the hips rather than swaying from side to side. We bring all the movements up to the womb, the **Sacral Chakra**. From there the waves just naturally emanate out. This will happen more and more as the body becomes more relaxed. In the beginning just focus on getting the movements to the hips and pelvic area (sacral chakra), the rest is a natural progression but we need to move into it gradually as the body softens and becomes more receptive to the movements and energy.

Allow the hip to move out to the side and up. As one hip is up the other has to be down, they are connected, then just lift the other hip. Think of going up and up. The one that is down goes up. It is easier to think of one movement, in one direction, rather than up and down. The down is a given since the hips are attached. Just focus on the pulling up. Because you are relaxed the other will automatically drop down.

The knees remain soft at all times. The feet remain in *wu chi*. If you move out of alignment begin again. Work through the knees. Use them to move the body but *never* straighten them. This may feel awkward at first as we are used to being pulled up, but the more you bend your joints the more flexibility you have—the more you will have a place to move into. If you are completely extended there is no place to go. Never allow your body to get into this position, of being completely extended and having nowhere to go.

Our joints are like the curves of the snake. They allow us to move. We may straighten one curve slightly but we then need to create another bend. When a snake is straight it cannot move. It needs to bend into its wave-like shape. It is the straightening and re-bending that allows the snake to move. We are trying to create the same perpetual motion. We can do this, like the snake, by alternating from side to side. If we are ever completely straight we are lost. There is no movement. We are over extended. Remember this concept the whole time you are Dancing. Keep everything relaxed and soft as much as possible.

Energy cannot flow through contracted muscles. This Dance is an energetic dance. Contraction is a masculine principle; flexibility and flow are the feminine principles. In ballet we are supposed to be pulled up, contracted, and controlled, here we are NOT. We initiate a movement, relax and see where it goes. Think of simply sitting all the time. In Egypt many of the best belly dancing teachers are old women. They teach sitting on a chair! It works.

Once you feel comfortable with the snake try some variations. Find some different rhythms in the music and follow them. Use this as an experiment in following the music. Let it guide and pull you. We are still only doing one movement, the snake, but we can find a lot of variety in that one movement. This is the best way to become comfortable with following the music. Use just one movement for a whole song but find the variations and follow them. This allows you to focus on the music rather than the movement, because it is the same movement over and over. This will push you to a place of *no-mind*. There is nothing to think about. Once you are in the movement it becomes perpetual. The body needs no more instruction.

Intensify the movement. Allow your body to curve and loosen more and more. You will feel awkward at first as though your body looks all bent and twisted. Resist your temptation to look in a mirror. The more bent and curved you are the more movement and energy is flowing through your body. Try to become as curved and relaxed as you can. Bend the knees more, lift the hip higher. The more exaggerated the movement the better you are doing it. In time this bending and twisting will become very comfortable and enjoyable. But first we need to break down the old walls.

Now it is time to move on to the **Air** movement. Here we are invoking the power of the **Bat**. Be sure you are standing in *wu chi*. The knees must be bent in order to remove any strain on the lower back. The shoulder blades are together, touching. Arms are down by your sides, light and ready to move. This position opens the **Heart Chakra**. If the knees are not bent in this position your buttocks will be sticking out and there will be stress on the lower back.

Stand in this position, arms light, and ready to move. Remain in this position until you connect with the music. When you feel it, like a gust of wind let the arms lift up, carried by that wind. Feel the air lifting your arms up and then gently allowing them to glide back down. The movement is simple up and down as if we are flying—flapping our wings.

Do not allow the shoulders to rise up. The movement originates from your shoulder blades, your "wing-bones". This movement, although simple, gets tiring very quickly. Your arms are much heavier than you realize. When your arms get tired, stop flying and shake them out. Shake out the shoulders and neck as well and then continue on. Stop as often as you need to. Do not push yourself beyond your limit. If the shoulders are coming up then it is too much stress, lower the arms. Do the same movement without letting the arms rise up as high. In time your wings will become stronger and you will be able to fly higher and longer. Don't push, just enjoy the flight.

Hear the different instruments in the music, the different rhythms. Fly with one for a while and then change and fly with another, as if you are catching one air current and then another. That is what eagles do. They find different currents and just ride from one to another, dancing with the air.

Now standing with arms open to the side almost shoulder height. Bring one hand into the chest, into the heart chakra, by bending at the elbow. Move as if you are scooping the air with your hand and bringing it in to the heart chakra. Then let the hand drop down and move out again to the side. Repeat the movement gathering more and more energy in the heart chakra. Now change hands and do it on the other side, gathering, scooping, and bringing in. Then alternate hands, one side and then the other. Allow the body to move in anyway it wants to. We are not attempting to make any other movement but at the same time we never stop the body from moving. The energy must be allowed to flow and move where it needs to.

From here we move on to **Water**. Begin by walking in a circle in time to the music. It is easier to do this movement walking than standing in place. Like water we are flowing. Walk in time to the music. Mark time by walking to the music. Be sure you are well synchronized with the music. As you are walking allow you body to become more and more relaxed. The knees bend more, the pelvis becomes softer. Feel yourself moving through space slowly and smoothly. Keep your steps very small. We want the movement to move through the body rather than being lost in space, in distance.

The body becomes more and more relaxed, soft knees, loose pelvis. The pelvis begins to rock forward and backward just from the movement, the walking. As the body becomes more and more relaxed the pelvis moves more deeply. We are moving like a **Fish** through water, allowing the waves to move through our body from our feet up through the body, forward and backward. As you become more relaxed the movement becomes stronger.

Now walk in place. The wave still moving through your body but you are not moving in space. Then plant both feet on the floor still allowing the wave to move through your body. You move like a mermaid forward and backward using you feet as fins. Because your feet are attached to the floor you need to really move through your feet and ankles to compensate.

Begin to walk in place again, just walking, listening to the music, synchronizing your movement to the beat. Now begin to walk backwards, taking small steps. Continue walking, feeling the music. Allow the body to become more and more relaxed. The knees become soft, the pelvis releases forward and backward. As you become more relaxed the movement increases. Feel yourself like a fish swimming through the water, undulating forward and backward. Feel the resistance from the water making it a very slow, very smooth, movement. Continue walking backward becoming more and more relaxed, moving more and more into the movement.

The last movement is the **Lion** and as I mentioned the most important movement. It represents the element of **Earth**. It is when we move from wave to vibration. Remember that the movement is initiated from your knees. It is not about moving your hips. Your hips will vibrate on their own from the force of the wave coming up through your knees.

When you begin the movement it will be slow and your hips *will* swing back and forth. Use the image of a cat before it strikes. It wiggles its rear-end back and forth. You want to attain that kind of looseness in your movement.

To start just bounce in place to the music. Use a heavy drum beat and just bounce. Then move into alternating movements—bending one knee and straightening, but never locking, the other. The knees must always remain soft. From here you have the movement. You will just increase the speed; remember the concepts of amplitude and frequency. As we speed up (frequency) the distance (amplitude) becomes smaller. We move from big movements to vibration as we increase speed.

If you get lost just begin again, from the bouncing. Once you get into the shimmy relax more and more. There is no end to the amount of relaxation you can attain. This is very important because the more relaxed the body is the more energy moves through. After time you may experience an opening of the **Root Chakra**. It is a wonderful experience. The feeling is like an explosion of heat. As if something was just released, with warmth, at your tail bone.

It may take some getting used to, not because of the movement but the sensation. Women these days tend to be locked in their hips. Often the feeling of having their buttocks shake is so unusual that they tense up and try to stop it. Everything is supposed to shake!

That will only increase the relaxation and the amount of energy that can move through you.

Remember that this Dance is an exercise in emptying yourself out in order to let that powerful Earth energy in. This is true empowerment, access to infinite power. The next step is to Dance all the movements together. Either moving from one movement to another or Dancing several of them together. Feel free to try everything and create **your** Dance.

Enjoy!

IN CONCLUSION

The movements I have suggested and taken you through are just the beginning, the base. From there you can build and create your Dance with infinite variations. This is where your own creativity steps in. Add turns, try different music. Try Dancing without music. Veils are a nice addition. You can use them to clear the aura or add color.

I believe that experiencing the Dance, with other women, is the best way to learn. I hope that this book will give you a greater insight into what is possible whether it is your first introduction to sacred dance, another layer to belly dancing or a form of dance that you are already doing.

At some point you may want to bring in the masculine energy. Dancing with a male is an incredible experience. Because of the power behind this Dance I caution you to do that in a sacred environment. The amount of energy moved for both parties is startling. I realized that I had never truly experienced male energy before having the experience of sacred dance with a male partner. The energy that moved through me was so *strong*—for lack of a better word. As the energy moved through me I felt like I was riding a bucking Bronco! The next morning I could hardly get out of bed my whole body was so sore. I truly had greater appreciation for males and their challenge to harness that energy after feeling it running through my own body.

As I mentioned, and my son suggested, this is only the beginning. From here I will continue to gather information. I hope to write another book on the next level of the tarot. I will use my website www.UniversalDancer.com to get that information out. I encourage you to write to me. I would love to hear your comments and experiences as well.

For me I have learned more from my students than I could have ever imagined. Teaching is an interactive process and my method of learning. I would love to learn from you.

I have already started to teach the second level of the tarot to a small group of people. And have had insights and pieces of the third level. This is one of the things that has encouraged me to write this book. I felt I needed to birth it to make space for what needs to come in next.

If you glance ahead the next card in the tarot is Strength—just to give you a clue. Doing this Dance and repeatedly having the experience of empowerment is the first step to real strength and lasting empowerment. In order to come into our power, Strength, we need to practice standing in that power until it becomes completely natural. At this point in time most people were raised with victim consciousness. We need to practice being empowered to know what that feels like—so that it becomes our default setting and we don't just fall back into victim mentality.

My real goal in writing this book and teaching workshops is to help women acquire a tool for connecting to that Divine power and the Divine/Universal feminine through the gift that was given to me—the gift of Dance.

I hope someday we will all have the opportunity to
Dance together!

GLOSSARY

Amplitude is a measurement of the oscillation of a wave. For our purposes in the Dance, it is simplified to the height or size of a wave.

Beginner's Mind is an eastern philosophy in which every new beginning is a new opportunity not based on previous experience or judgment.

Caduceus is commonly known as "the staff of Hermes". It is an esoteric symbol representing the Serpent Goddess in her duality. It also represents the Indian concept of the Kundalini, the two serpents being the Ida and the Pingala.

Chakra is a Sanskrit word meaning "spinning wheel". Chakras are vortices of energy in the body. The chakras system is the most common nomenclature used in healing modalities to express specific energy centers. Each one lies over an endocrine gland, funneling energy into the body and activating the gland. The chakras have correspondences in different senses and aspects such as color, musical note, taste, etc.

Coherence is the balance between order and chaos (from Lynn McTaggart's *The Field*)—the point we strive for embracing both aspects. Order brings in structure, chaos creativity—we need them both.

Collective Unconscious a term Carl Jung used for the unconscious mind, the place where all the archetypes reside. It could also be thought of what we now call "the field" or "the zero point field", the wave-field of space around us.

Entrainment is when a group is resonating or pulsating together. It is why women living together begin to menstruate together, or clocks in a shop begin to tick together. It is also what happens between mother and child when their hearts begin to beat together. We can use entrainment consciously to assist each other in the movements.

Fibonacci Sequence is a series of numbers. The sequence is created when numbers are added in a specific fashion. Two numbers are added, then the product of those numbers is added to the second number in the equation—such as $0+1=1$, $1+1=2$, $1+2=3$, $2+3=5$.... This is done infinitely, creating the sequence (1,2,3,5...). When this sequence is plotted on a graph it creates a spiral, Phi (see below). This spiral is found in nature in all types and forms such as the conch shell, hurricanes, flowers etc. In esoteric wisdom it is seen as Divine Unfolding where *the past + the present = the future*.

Frequency is the number of waves over a specified distance.

Hat-hor was the very ancient Egyptian goddess/*neter* of love, beauty and empowerment. She represents the Divine Feminine, the mother archetype and the sacred cow. With Sekhmet, she comprises the two aspects of the Serpent Goddess. After the Age of Aries, and the onset of patriarchy, she was pushed aside and almost forgotten. Her name means "house of Horus" or "womb of the Hero".

Horus was the *neter* representing the "hero" or the "prodigal son" archetype in ancient Egypt. He became more prevalent and significant in patriarchal times.

Invoke is to bring in. It is the conscious act of calling in a specific energy. We can invoke the energy of the Divine Feminine or a power animal in order to use that energy—pass it through our bodies.

Isis represented the archetype of the High Priestess. She was a priestess of Hat-hor, the Divine Feminine/Serpent Goddess. Her role as messenger of the goddess was to bring those energies to

Earth. With the rise of the Sun god Ra, the patriarchy, and the separation of the Serpent Goddesses, the brother-sister *neteru* (Isis/Osiris Nephthys/Set) rose to prominence.

Kundalini is the energy channel running through the body in Indian philosophy. It consists of two serpents, the Ida and the Pingala, and a tube the Sushumna. Symbolically it is represented by the caduceus.

Marking time is aligning to the beat. Before we begin any Dance we stand in *wu chi* and align ourselves to the music. We allow the beat to become our own internal rhythm so that we move together with the waves of the music.

Medium is a base or the substrate that a wave moves through or over. In the case of the Dance the medium is our body—specifically the fluid parts of our body that are permeable.

Natural Frequency is the intrinsic rhythm of a given object or medium. Everything has it's own natural frequency. When that rhythm is attained, the system will collapse. This is why soldiers are taught to break step when crossing a bridge. If the natural frequency of a bridge was attained by the soldiers marching—the bridge would collapse. This is also the principle behind healing with homeopathy and Trager. The system (body) is hit with energy over and over again or rocked—when it reaches it's natural frequency the system collapses and the dysfunctional program/wave pattern is broken and healing occurs.

Neter (neteru pl.) means archetype or aspect of nature. The word dates back to the Pharaonic times and was mistranslated by Egyptologists to mean "god". The ancient Egyptian language had no vowels (like most Middle Eastern languages) so the original hieroglyphic characters represented were *ntr*, which when vowels are added, becomes the word "nature" in almost every language.

No-mind is a contradictory state of being. It is the point where we are complexly present and absent at the same moment. We are grounded, fully present with in ourselves, while being completely connected to the cosmos at the same time.

Numinous is the Divine realm—the unknowable, unseen, but ever present realm. We can feel the numinous—the presence of the Divine but it is hard to explain.

Nut was the Sky goddess/*neter* in the ancient Egyptian mythology. She was a consort of Geb, the Earth god/*neter*.

Ouroboros is the alchemic symbol of the snake eating its own tail. The symbol represents transformation, death and rebirth, the phoenix rising from the ashes after being consumed.

Phi is a mathematical symbol (as well as a Greek letter) representing a fraction. In esoteric wisdom it represents our path or Divine unfolding. We each have our own unique Phi, our individual unfolding. Because it is a fraction, it is dynamic. It shows a relationship between points of events. Even though the points on the spiral are unique to each individual, the shape of the spiral is the same, like a conch shell or sunflower.

Power Animals are best known from the Native American tradition but present in many cultures—especially shamanic cultures. Animals are the third dimension or level of evolution. Although they can move through space, unlike minerals (the first dimension) or plants (the second dimension), which are stationary, they still retain group (pack) consciousness. This means that their movements and messages are consistent throughout the species. When a power animal comes to you in person or in a dream, they have a specific message for you. Shamanic cultures use these animal messengers to guide them. We can also invoke the energy of power animals to enhance the Dance or our movements.

Sacred Marriage is a stage of the alchemical process. It is the union of opposites—when the "Black King" unites with the "White Queen". It is the point of integration or fusion. Psychoanalyst Carl Jung popularized the concept. He explained it as a point in our lives, usually around the age or 40 (or the Uranus Opposition see below), when we integrate the two polarities (masculine and feminine) within ourselves.

Serpent Goddess is an ancient (and modern) deity. The serpent goddess represents the primordial wave. Her presence can often be experience during altered states of consciousness such as ecstatic experience or the use of sacred plants such as Ayahuasca. There are two aspects of the Serpent Goddess. She is known by many names, including the Attractive/Assertive goddess or the kundalini. In the very ancient Pharaonic times she was Hat-hor/Sekhmet.

Surrender is the state of releasing control to the Divine. It is what we search for on the road to bliss and what the last card in the tarot, the World, Universe or Universal Dance, represents. It is the point when we move in Divine harmony.

Trager Approach is a type of bodywork used to release physical and mental patterns. Milton Trager, M.D, developed it. The practitioner moves the body with gentle rhythmic movements until the body reaches the "natural frequency" (see above) and releases. It is similar to the Dance where we use rhythmic wave patterns to help the body release dysfunctional patterns and come back into harmony.

Uranus Opposition occurs when the planet Uranus is exactly opposite its position in the natal astrological chart. This aspect occurs to everyone between the ages of 38 and 42, depending on where Uranus is in the chart. It is the point where we integrate both the feminine and masculine aspects of ourselves. It is the point that Carl Jung called the Sacred Marriage (see above). If we can navigate this period well, then "life begins at 40". If not, then we may have a "mid-life crisis".

Virgin was traditionally a symbol of purity and totality. It described "the woman (or man) who is complete in herself (himself)". Only later did it become a word to describe someone who had never experienced sexual intercourse.

Wu chi is the position we begin the Dance in. It is also used in Chinese martial arts where the word *wu chi* means "potential" and *tai chi* means "form". It is the point before we move where we build our potential through stillness.

FURTHER READING

Andrews, Ted. *Animal Speak: The Spiritual & Magical Powers of Creatures Great & Small*. St. Paul, MN: Llewellyn Publications, 2003.

Clow, Barbara Hand. *Liquid Light of Sex: Understanding Your Key Life Passages*. Santa Fe, NM: Bear & Pub., 1991.

Eliade, Mircea. *The Sacred and the Profane: The Nature of Religion*. New York: Harcourt, Brace & World, 1959.

Hay, Louise L. *You Can Heal Your Life*. Carlsbad, CA: Hay House, 1999.

Judith, Anodea. *Eastern Body, Western Mind: Psychology and the Chakra System as a Path to the Self*. Berkeley, CA: Celestial Arts, 1996.

McTaggart, Lynne. *The Field: The Quest for the Secret Force of the Universe*. New York: Harper, 2002.

Myss, Caroline M. *Sacred Contracts: Awakening Your Divine Potential*. New York: Three Rivers Press, 2003.

Qualls-Corbett, Nancy. *The Sacred Prostitute: Eternal Aspect of the Feminine*. Toronto, Canada: Inner City Books, 1988.

Shapiro, Debbie. *The BodyMind Workbook: Exploring How the Mind and the Body Work Together*. Shaftesbury, Dorset: Element, 1990.

ABOUT THE AUTHOR

Leslie Zehr left Western culture in 1986 to make her home in Egypt. Based on her experiences in Egypt she has developed her unique method of teaching dance and esoteric wisdom. In 2002 she received an initiation in Upper Egypt. It was at that time that she began receiving the information on the *Universal Dancer*. She spent twenty years serving the goddess Hat-hor in a modern-day temple in Cairo—the Centre for Sacred Arts.

Most of Leslie's time is spent developing the Greater Work of the *Universal Dancer* through personal experience and teaching. She lectures and teaches workshops internationally on Sacred Dance, the Universal Dancer, and The Essences of Egypt.

Leslie is a Hypnotherapist and Reiki Master; with international certifications in Homeopathy, Touch for Health, and Aromatherapy, a certificate in Sandplay therapy and a B.S. in Psychology from Virginia Tech, where she also studied biochemistry.

Her Shamanic work with plants has led her to develop the Alchemia Remedies; a line of Egyptian Flower and Sacred Sites Remedies which hold the energy of Egypt herself. They can be used for transformational and alchemical healing.

In addition to the book *The Alchemy of Dance* (in English and Spanish), she has published *The Sacred Art of Dance Journal*, *The Alchemia Remedies: Vibrational Essences from Egyptian Flowers and Sacred Sites*, a CD entitled *Navel Portal Activation and Guided Visualizations* and numerous articles on Sacred Dance, Alchemy and Aromatherapy.

Leslie continues to reside in Egypt. For more information visit Leslie at www.UniversalDancer.com.